LE CALVAIRE

Contents

Cover: France hovers terrified between the Soviet fist and the Nazi maw—1937 cartoon
Front endpaper: France suffers on the cross of depression, 1934
Rear endpaper: 'But France has not lost the war . . .'—General and Madame de Gaulle in London after the fall of France

Copyright © 1972: Wilfrid Knapp
First published in 1972 by Macdonald
St Giles House 49 Poland St London W1
in the British Commonwealth and
American Heritage Press
The Rockefeller Center New York
in the United States of America
Library of Congress Catalogue Card
Number: 74-37951 12 –13– 73
Made and printed in Great Britain by
Purnell & Sons Ltd Paulton Somerset

FRANCE: PARTIAL ECLIPSE

From the Stavisky Riots to the Nazi Conquest

Wilfrid Knapp

Library of the 20th Century
Macdonald/American Heritage Press

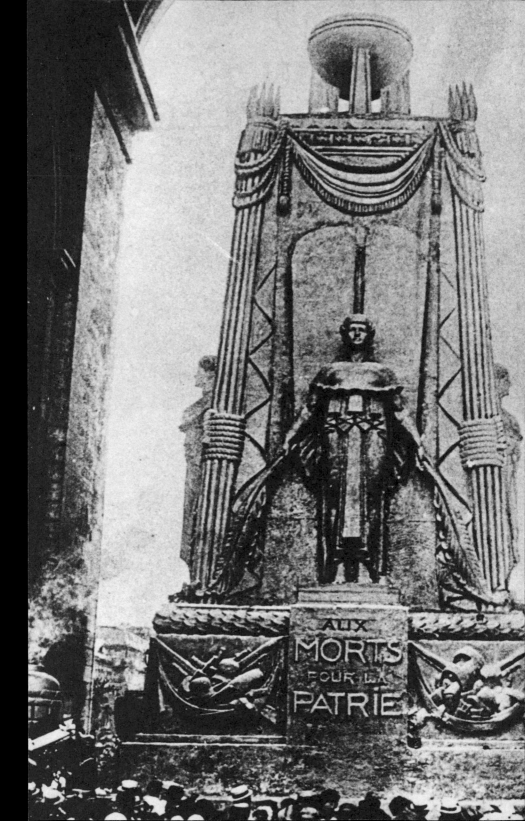

AUX
MORTS
POUR LA
PATRIE

France: Divided and Defensive

Historically France has been the microcosm of Europe. The conflicts which have torn Europe apart have severed France; ideological debate has been concentrated and intensified within the French political community. When Europe was at its lowest ebb during the Second World War France lay prostrate; the resurgence of Europe was closely related to the contribution of France to the European Movement.

But the period which preceded the Second World War was one when the creative genius of France was dormant. A secular change had occurred at the beginning of the century. Until then France was the originator of much of the dynamics of Europe: but after 1900, for fifty years, it suffered the conflict of forces, not of its own choosing but imposed from outside.

In the 16th century the religious wars, for all that they cost in tearing society apart, had produced the political thought of Jean Bodin, who gave the first modern interpretation of the concept of sovereignty in the state. In the 17th century came the glamour of the court of Louis XIV. With the collapse of the Bourbon monarchy, the importance of France to the historical development of Europe reached its height. The issues of the Revolution were the central questions of authority and liberty, of ideology and tolerance, of religion and secular rule. The Revolution completed the unification of France and at the same time invoked the rise of nationalism across the continent of Europe. It plunged Europe into the conflict of the Napoleonic wars and left the Napoleonic code of law as its permanent memorial.

The 20th-century experience of France was very different from this. The experience which had the deepest impact on French society was the First World War — a catastrophic conflict which began as a struggle for power and ended with a flourish of idealism, indispensable, it

Left: *Memorial to the 1,400,000 Frenchmen killed in the First World War — sorrow over the losses in that conflict, and a desire to avoid another, were dominating themes in the political and cultural life of France throughout the decade of the 1930s*

5

seemed, for sustaining the courage of the fatigued and battling nations. The war was not of French making. French diplomacy, designed to protect France from the growing might of Germany, added to the tension which exploded in 1914. But the war was one imposed on France. As a result some 1,400,000 people were killed — one man for every twenty-eight men, women, and children in the whole population. But when victory was won and the invading armies had been expelled, the international problems of France returned. In population and industrial strength France was weak in relation to Germany. At the same time the destruction of the European political system to the east of Germany made more difficult the construction of a balance of power favourable to France.

The war had an indirect effect which was even more long-lasting. It imposed a burden on the Tsarist government of Russia greater than the country could sustain, and so opened the way to the ideological drive and the ruthless determination of Lenin and the Bolsheviks. The Communist Revolution established a new regime which Stalin was able to consolidate into a durable totalitarian order. To the historical absolutism of Russia was now welded an ideology which claimed universal validity and which attracted the disciplined commitment of men who found a new faith in Communism.

The Bolshevik Revolution was no more of French making than the war. But it divided the labour movement of France as of the rest of Europe. More than that, it invoked the loyalty of men to international Communism rather than to their own country.

In the 1930s Europe's conflicts were, once again, identical with those within France. But France was the unwilling victim rather than the creative, moving spirit. The war had drained the lifeblood of the country; the Bolshevik Revolution had created a new ideological centre in Moscow. In Italy and Germany nationalism now acquired a new, virulent, aggressive force in the radical destructiveness of Fascism and Nazism. Fascism found its admirers and imitators in France. It joined forces with those who hankered after a traditional order of things and looked back to monarchic rule; in so doing it sapped the strength of the nation.

Economically and socially too France was divided. The country's wealth was concentrated in its northern half — in the region around Paris and in the industrial areas of the north and north-east. In this area the slow reconstruction which had been undertaken after the First

Right: The instability of successive governments in the inter-war period led to profound disenchantment with the system

Chronological list of Premiers of the Third Republic from 1917 to 1940

Year	Premier (figure denotes 1st, 2nd, 3rd etc. ministry)	Date of nomination	Date of termination
1917			
	Clemenceau 2	16 November 1917	18 January 1920
1918			
1919			
1920	Millerand 1	20 January 1920	18 February 1920
	Millerand 2	18 February 1920	23 September 1920
	Leygues	24 September 1920	12 January 1921
1921	Briand 7	16 January 1921	12 January 1922
1922	Poincaré 2	15 January 1922	26 March 1924
1923			
1924	Poincaré 3	29 March 1924	1 June 1924
	François—Marsal	9 June 1924	13 June 1924
	Herriot 1	14 June 1924	10 April 1925
1925	Painlevé 2	17 April 1925	27 October 1925
	Painlevé 3	29 October 1925	22 November 1925
	Briand 8	28 November 1925	6 March 1926
1926	Briand 9	9 March 1926	15 June 1926
	Briand 10	23 June 1926	17 July 1926
	Herriot 2	19 July 1926	21 July 1926
	Poincaré 4	23 July 1926	6 November 1928
1927			
1928			
	Poincaré 5	11 November 1928	27 July 1929
1929			
	Briand 11	29 July 1929	29 October 1929
	Tardieu 1	3 November 1929	17 February 1930
1930	Chautemps 1	21 February 1930	25 February 1930
	Tardieu 2	2 March 1930	4 December 1930
	Steeg	13 December 1930	22 January 1931
1931	Laval 1	27 January 1931	13 June 1931
	Laval 2	13 June 1931	12 January 1932
1932	Laval 3	14 January 1932	16 February 1932
	Tardieu 3	20 February 1932	10 May 1932
	Herriot 3	3 June 1932	14 December 1932
	Paul Boncour	18 December 1932	28 January 1933
1933	Daladier	31 January 1933	24 October 1933
	Sarraut 1	26 October 1933	24 November 1933
	Chautemps 2	26 November 1933	27 January 1934
1934	Daladier 2	30 January 1934	7 February 1934
	Doumergue 2	9 February 1934	8 November 1934
	Flandin	8 November 1934	30 May 1935
1935	Bouisson	1 June 1935	4 June 1935
	Laval 4	7 June 1935	23 January 1936
1936	Sarraut 2	24 January 1936	3 June 1936
	Blum 1	4 June 1936	21 June 1937
1937	Chautemps 3	22 June 1937	14 January 1938
1938	Chautemps 4	18 January 1938	10 March 1938
	Blum 2	13 March 1938	8 April 1938
	Daladier 3	10 April 1938	20 March 1940
1939			
1940	Reynaud	21 March 1940	16 June 1940
	Pétain	17 June 1940	**July 10 1940** **Assembly votes full constitutional powers to Marshal Pétain. End of the Third Republic.**

World War had created a modern industrial sector. South
of the Loire the picture was different. Agriculture pro-
gressed slowly, and there was little incentive or natural
resources for the development of industry. The major
towns and ports—Lyons, Marseilles, Bordeaux—were
centres of modern economic life. But in the countryside
growth did not keep pace with that of the northern
departments. For the visitor the aspect of rural France
retained all its charm—the villages and country towns,
the timeless sequence of the agricultural seasons, clear
mountain air and limpid streams, Mass in crumbling
village churches or *pastis* in the café.

But for the more perceptive observer the mood of the
countryside was much less joyful. After the Second World
War the census was to show that the average age of rural
houses was 120 years. Although modern conveniences in
the countryside did improve slowly only 34 per cent of
peasant homes had running water—even though 90 per
cent had electricity—in 1934. The men who lived in these
homes included many of those who had fought in the First
World War—although a proportion of those who survived
joined the steady drift from the countryside to the towns
and the richer areas of the north. The twenty years that
had passed since then brought little reward for the sacrifice which was commemorated on the war memorials of
every village. The boom of the war years soon ended—in
any case, it had not improved the peasant's position rela-
tive to the rest of the country, given the general increase
in prices. The slump which came in 1932-4 widened still
further the gap between town and country. Prices fell—
but the price paid to the farmer suffered the sharpest fall
of all, much sharper than the price of food in towns and
the price of manufactured goods. The natural reaction
of peasants and politicians was defensive. The sense of
frustration and resentment towards the France of the
cities and the capital grew proportionately.

A defensive mentality
But there too defence was the dominant mood, broken
only by the short-lived enthusiasm of the Popular Front,
which came to power in 1936. The modern sector of the
economy produced only one great monument of construction in this period. It was not a dam, or a reservoir,
or some new constructive enterprise—it was the defensive barrier of the Maginot Line, paid for by public funds,
involving no risk, and symbolising the fearfulness with
which France defended itself from the dangers of the
outside world.

In literature and the arts the record is more impressive;
but even here the 1930s produced relatively few new
departures. Outstanding amongst those writers who

⁵ produced some of their best work in this decade was
François Mauriac, who was elected to the Académie
Française in 1933. He had already published *Thérèse
Desqueyroux* (1927) and *Le Nœud de vipères* (1932). His
novels continued to show a preoccupation with the Christian themes of sin and redemption underlying personal,
particularly family relationships. *Les Anges noirs* and
Les Chemins de la mer appeared before the war, *La
Pharisienne* in 1941.

Mauriac was also deeply concerned with the political
conflicts of the period. He was passionately opposed to
totalitarianism in all its forms and wrote polemically
against Fascism at the time of the Ethiopian campaign
⁶ and the Spanish Civil War. He shared this distinction
with another Catholic writer, Georges Bernanos—a
visionary with an immediate sense of the forces of good
and evil. Isolated, like Mauriac, from the majority of his
fellow Catholics he was unsparing in his denunciation of
what he regarded as religious hypocrisy, particularly in
Spain. At the same time he wrote his most popular work,
Journal d'un curé de campagne, published in 1936.

In the last years before the war a new school of thought
took birth. Concerned with the role of the individual in an
apparently purposeless world Jean-Paul Sartre began to
express his existentialist philosophy, which had its full
⁷ impact when the war was over—*La Nausée* appeared in
the year of the Munich agreement. Jean Cocteau continued his experimentation in all forms of art—*Les
Parents terribles* following *Les Enfants terribles,* both of
which were later to be made into films. Meanwhile Jean
Renoir was diverting to the cinema the artistic talent
inherited from his father and produced, in *La Règle du
Jeu,* a film as important for its social commentary as for
its beauty.

Amongst intellectuals of the Left there was no respite
from the political problems which were of immediate importance to the content if not to the style of their writing.
They had seen a new world come into being in Soviet
⁸ Russia, only to be confronted with the moral problems
arising from the Moscow state trials, the Spanish Civil
War, and the change of Communist policy which came
with the signature of the Nazi-Soviet pact in 1939.
Romain Rolland, writing in the Communist paper
L'Humanité, was deeply concerned with the fate of poli-

Left: *Luminaries of French culture during the thirties—1.
Catholic writer Georges Bernanos; 2. Famous novelist Colette
in 1939; 3. Writer André Malraux; 4. Composer Darius Milhaud;
5. Novelist and poet Louis Aragon; 6. Poet Jean Cocteau; 7.
Avant-garde composer and songwriter François Poulenc; 8.
Louis Jouvet—theatre director and greatest actor of his day*

tical prisoners; Louis Aragon's poetry was infused with his political preoccupations.

Their language inevitably lacked the universality of painting, and the most widely known monument to the period was Picasso's *Guernica,* inspired by the bombardment which German aeroplanes carried out during the Spanish Civil War. Picasso, a Spaniard who made his home in France, found a freedom there which did not exist in his own native country. But much of the impetus and stimulus which made Paris a centre for artists had died away—its pre-eminence was never to be regained.

For a while France had lost the self-confidence of its nationalism. In the 1880s French schoolboys still read the history of the country in the romantic epic of Jules Michelet—a republican historian whose life spanned the first three-quarters of the 19th century. The struggles and victories of Joan of Arc, the storming of the Bastille, the great unifying force of the Revolution formed a continuous whole in his eloquent panegyric. But the schoolbooks of the 1920s were written under the impact of the war, and even when they celebrated victory they ranged from a virulent denunciation of Germany to a defensive picture of France.

In the 1930s the danger from outside reappeared. By the time the slump was reaching its nadir in France it had already produced its dire political consequences in Germany with Hitler's advent to power. François-Poncet, the French ambassador to Berlin, used the Christmas holiday in 1933 to write a despatch summarising the change which had swept across Germany. 'Few revolutions, in the history of Europe,' he wrote, 'have met less obstacle than that of the Hitlerites. Few revolutions have more easily destroyed their opponents and conquered an entire country. It was like a tidal wave breaking, like a fire blown by the wind.'

François-Poncet's countrymen did not have to share his informed and analytical view to have the same sense of alarm about Hitler's rise to power. For them it represented a resurgence of a Germany they believed they knew only too well. Even so the dangers to the nation seemed to come not only from across the Rhine but from inside the country as well.

Right: *A new architecture for new materials—the main front of the Salvation Army Hostel in Paris, designed by Le Corbusier*

Haute Couture

In the 1930s Paris retained and even strengthened its primacy in the world of fashion. The simple, angular, 'masculine' fashions of the 1920s had not really utilised the special flair of the great French houses (as, indeed, they had not particularly favoured the customarily generous proportions of French womanhood), and the designers of New York and London had made inroads upon the preserves of their Paris colleagues. But the intricate, feminine fashions of the 1930s were ideal for the talents of both French women and French designers. The international buyers flocked to the re-invigorated Paris fashion shows (see the open-air showing on the **right**). One element of great interest was the close link between certain Paris designers and the world of fine arts. The creations of the great Coco Chanel (**below**) particularly benefited from her friendships with such *avant garde* artists as Picasso and Jean Cocteau, and were integral to the artistic milieu of the time

Chapter 1
6th February

The five years which preceded the Second World War opened, in France, with riots in the centre of Paris. The date, 6th February 1934, acquired the evocative quality of other major landmarks of French history — *le quatorze juillet, le quat'septembre, le seize mai.* It was a date of bad memory which never became a street name.

On the evening of that day organised right-wing bands of demonstrators tried to cross the bridge from the Place de la Concorde to the Chamber of Deputies. As they did so there were bursts of gunfire which killed fifteen, while hundreds amongst both the police and the demonstrators were injured. Violence on this scale had not been seen since the suppression of the Commune in 1871.

The immediate cause of the riots of 6th February was the traditional one of government corruption. In December 1933 the news broke of the exploits of a swindler who had enjoyed the protection of the police and the judiciary. The experience was not novel in the history of the Third Republic, which had, before 1914, seen the sale of honours by the son-in-law of the President and the widespread involvement of deputies in the misappropriation of funds intended for the construction of the Panama canal.

On 8th January 1934 Serge-Alexandre Stavisky was found dead, shot through the temple, in a Chamonix chalet. By birth he was Russian and Jewish, the son of a dentist from the town of Sobodka. In 1900 he was naturalised, and so acquired French citizenship — but citizenship which left him vulnerable to the intolerant and racist elements of French nationalism. His career, moreover, provided plenty of material for those who wanted to believe that foreign immigrants sapped the French character and threatened to destroy French society. He was a confidence trickster and swindler who had remained at liberty through a long career of misappropriating other people's money because he could always find friends in the police, the judiciary, and parliament who were ready to help him. He had acquired his expensive habits while young—in 1909 he was left with a swindle on his hands by his grandfather, who had emigrated with all the family from the Ukraine, and had escaped from his embarrassment with the help of Albert Clemenceau, brother of the 'Tiger'. He made money during the First World War while others lost their lives, and was only arrested in 1925 over a particularly blatant affair of a false cheque. But the incriminating evidence disappeared from the desk of the police inspector, and a fortnight was the full extent of Stavisky's sojourn in prison. Arrested for a more rewarding swindle, he was released to have an appendix operation; but when he returned to freedom, his appendix ceased even to grumble and Stavisky was able to remain in 'provisional liberty', engineering successively more grandiose swindles. Eventually it was a modest local government officer who discovered the fraudulent issue of bonds on the municipal pawnshop of Bayonne which led to his downfall.

Government corruption

A swindle would not by itself have brought the riots; it was the connivance of men in government which produced the feeling which was expressed on the boulevards and in the Place de la Concorde. The police too were discredited—and they lacked reserves of credit on which to draw. Stavisky's death occurred after the police had discovered his hideout (which was not very intelligently concealed). They searched the chalet in a way which made it easy for him to commit suicide—and in a way which left it open for the Right to claim that he had been murdered by the police, or by the police under orders from the Premier.

Meanwhile, every day that passed after the first revelation of Stavisky's career on 28th December 1933 brought additional sensations. After all it was scarcely possible to obtain nineteen adjournments of a trial over a period of years without the exercise of influence in the right places. Two Radical deputies, Joseph Garat and Gaston Bonnaure, had been bought by Stavisky to protect his interests. His lawyers included prominent Radical politicians. In addition the scale of his operation was such as to include a wide range of deputies, ministers, judges, police officers, and newspaper proprietors. The full extent of complicity was difficult to judge with accuracy; its very uncertainty made it more damning to parliament as a whole and above all to the Radical Party. The Premier, Camille Chautemps, added to the strength of rumour and

Right: French art in the thirties—Raoul Dufy's vision of the electrical age, part of a fresco in the Electricity Pavilion at the 1937 Paris World Fair. Next page: 'The Nude in the Bath' (1937) by the painter Pierre Bonnard. Page 20: 'The Blue Spider' (1938) by Fernand Leger, from the ultramodern school of art

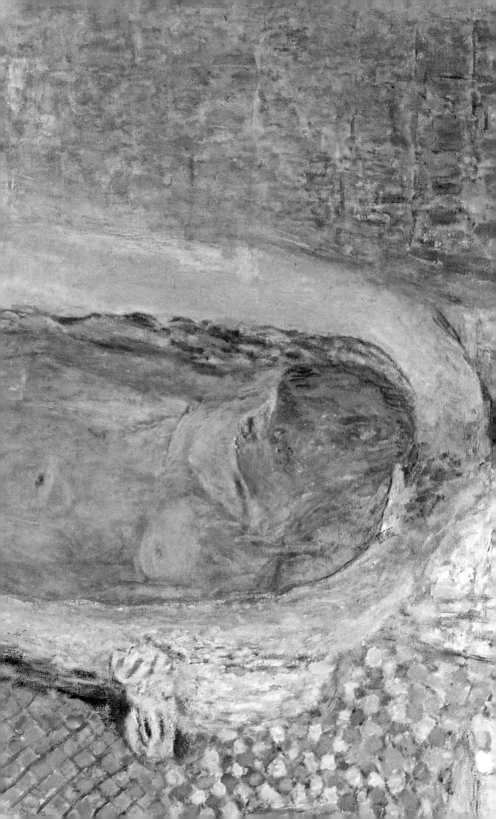

accusation by refusing to appoint a committee of enquiry; one of his own ministers, Albert Dalimier, was implicated. In the streets right-wing bands demonstrated violently in what was to be a prelude to the 6th February. Chautemps took the easy way out and resigned.

He was succeeded by another of the luminaries of the Radical Party — Edouard Daladier. It was his task to defend the Republic. There was little that was radical in the ideology of the French Radical Party, but the maintenance of the parliamentary system of government, in which the Party had come to play a dominant and central role, was of paramount importance to it. His task was not easy. The discrediting of the Republic came primarily from members of his own party who had been unmindful enough of public responsibilities to profit from the Stavisky empire. His predecessor had resigned as a result of attacks from younger members of their own party intent on seeing that justice should be done. His own appointment to the premiership was viewed with great ill-will by his outstanding rival, Edouard Herriot, who thought that the office should have gone to him.

Daladier had the reputation of being a strong man — it proved to be the most bogus reputation of the interwar years. He was, and continued to be, untouched by the Stavisky scandal. With an impressive if not distinguished war record he might hope to command the respect of the ex-servicemen's organisations which had been responsible for sporadic rioting over the past weeks. His first task was to form a government and ensure that it was supported in the Chamber. Unable to find enough votes in the Centre he looked for them to the Left and was willing to pay a price for them — though he gravely underestimated what he was doing. He dismissed a man who had become a *bête noire* of the Socialists — Jean Chiappe, the head of the Paris police.

The operation was a clumsy one. Chiappe had the reputation of enforcing harsh repression of Communist demonstrations and showing a gentler touch with the Right; his dismissal therefore might win points for Daladier in the game of politics as it was practised in the Chamber of Deputies. But Chiappe was a colourful figure — he had done much to stop soliciting in the streets and had introduced the famous metal stud pedestrian crossings as well as creating an 'image' of himself by dressing in a top hat and silk scarf. His dismissal made him a martyr and provided the pretext for the riots of 6th February.

The riots took the form of an uncoordinated attempt to break through police barricades to the Palais Bourbon, where the Chamber of Deputies was in session. There was little originality in the minds of those who so acted — men of the Right were taking over a tradition of the Left, for

ever since 1791 it had been the customary procedure of demonstrators to invade the Chamber. Daladier eventually resigned, in spite of having secured a majority in the Chamber, and thus gave his government the dubious honour of being the first since 1848 to be overthrown by a revolt in the streets.

To intelligent men observing the events of 6th February the scene was full of danger. Men devoted to freedom and democracy saw the Assembly building as a symbol of parliamentary government and believed that if government was overthrown there it would pass into the streets. The situation of the Palais Bourbon, now the National Assembly, added to their sense of crisis. The main onslaught of the demonstrators was from the Place de la Concorde towards the bridge, and it was the bridge which the police held, like Horatius and his brothers (although more numerous). On the left bank a subsidiary demonstration led by Colonel de la Rocque was turned back by a thinner defensive line in the Rue de Bourgogne.

No one was more impressed by the risks being run than the Socialist leader, Léon Blum. After the war he testified to a parliamentary committee of enquiry about the events of the pre-war days and urged that the sense of the ridiculous which came with relief immediately after the event was misleading. 'The Sixth of February was a redoubtable attempt against the Republic,' he said. Only a handful of *gardes mobiles* prevented the dispersal of government and deputies from the Chamber – when 'a provisional government would have been proclaimed', as had happened on the 4th September 1870.

Blum was probably wrong in his analysis of the dangers; but his diagnosis is understandable. As Daladier wavered and proposed resignation, Blum had offered to enter the government to increase its authority – taking on himself the responsibility of abandoning the established practice of the Socialist Party not to participate in a government until they could lead it. He sought to give the legitimate government of France the determination the King of Italy had lacked in failing to order the disbandment of Mussolini's Fascist gangs. He, like François-Poncet, had seen the bewildering speed of the destruction of German institutions over the previous year and judged the danger to France accordingly.

It was no dictator who followed Daladier. It was not easy to find a replacement, after both Chautemps and Daladier had accepted defeat. President Lebrun looked for a man who stood above party conflict, who would be quickly accepted and able to form a government without dangerous delay. He sent to the small town of Tourne-

Left: The swindler Stavisky after his suicide – or was it murder?

23

feuille in the south where a former President of the Republic, Gaston Doumergue, was living in retirement. Madame Doumergue had hastily to repack their suitcases — they were just setting out to Egypt on the 7th February. Instead they took the train to Paris where they were met by some three hundred people, chief amongst them President Lebrun and former President Poincaré.

Doumergue was eminently acceptable to the Centre of the Chamber — including the Radicals, who offered their support. He was indeed an old republican and a freemason who, until then, had distinguished himself more by his mediocre acceptance of the rules of Third Republic politics than anything else. He was much less acceptable to the Left — there was no question of Blum's readiness to join Daladier's embattled government being extended to Doumergue's cabinet of National Union.

Instead the Socialists outside the Chamber now joined with the Communists in a counter-demonstration to that of 6th February. On the 12th a general strike was called and massive demonstrations were organised. Nervously the new government watched what it regarded as a new threat to order. But there was no mishap in Paris — though elsewhere, especially in Marseilles, the demonstrators and the police succeeded in wounding each other. The demonstration was nonetheless impressive. Léon Blum, Vincent Auriol, Paul Faure (Secretary of the Socialist Party) led the crowd, chanting 'Unity of Action, Unity of Action!' They were followed by the Communist leaders, Marcel Cachin and Jacques Duclos, heading a column chanting the *Internationale* and other revolutionary songs. The struggle against Fascism was the order of the day — that and the defence of the Republic. It was the beginning of the Popular Front, which eventually was to unite Socialists, Radicals, and Communists.

In the Chamber business was conducted in a more normal manner — which did not prevent the Communist deputies from calling Doumergue 'Murderer' when he took the rostrum. The budget was passed. Two committees were established to enquire into the events which had brought the government of National Union to power — one to investigate the Stavisky affair, the other the events of 6th February. More popularly they were known respectively as the 'Thieves' Committee' and the 'Murderers' Committee'. Their enquiry produced plentiful opportunity for continuing effervescence in the Press as the more notable witnesses, like Chiappe, were called and the more outstanding politicians on the edge of the affair were questioned. But in the end their proceedings tailed off as had happened with many previous commissions of

Left: A victim of the violent street-fighting of February 1934

a similar sort, without it being obvious that justice had been done. Gradually the events ceased to dominate parliamentary life. The government became more concerned with the renewed decline of the economy. Doumergue's advent to power had had a temporary effect of restoring confidence; but by itself it was not enough to solve the problems of economic depression. As industrial production declined and unemployment increased there was a generalised defensive reaction to safeguard the value of the franc – so recently stabilised by Poincaré. The Finance Minister, Germain-Martin, expressed his opposition to devaluation in the moral terms which were so prevalent in economic debate: 'To devalue the franc would be to break the most sacred contract. What the state promises is a fixed weight of gold. To devalue is bankruptcy, is systematic failure.'

The Chamber also found time to take up the possibility of constitutional reform. A committee elaborated a series of reforms which included a proposal that the President of the Republic should be given real power to dissolve the Chamber.

The possibility of such measures being enacted was very slight. But they were taken up by Gaston Doumergue, who began to behave in a manner which alarmed and frightened the good Republicans who had welcomed him to office. Speaking to the Chamber of Deputies he caused a stir when he expressed his belief that the great majority of the country wanted constitutional reform and that it belonged 'to the French people, to the country and the country alone, sovereign in a democracy, to take such a decision'.

There was worse to come. Doumergue discovered radio. He began to broadcast, and not only to broadcast but to talk on the radio about possible changes in the constitution – the strengthening of the premiership by the establishment of a premier's office independent of the departmental ministries, and the setting up of a consultative economic council.

Alarmed by this apparent bid to strengthen the executive power the Radical Party withdrew its support from the Doumergue cabinet. Edouard Herriot used the issue as a means of reasserting his dominance over the party, which he had lost under Daladier's premiership, and at the beginning of November 1934 led the resignations from the Cabinet.

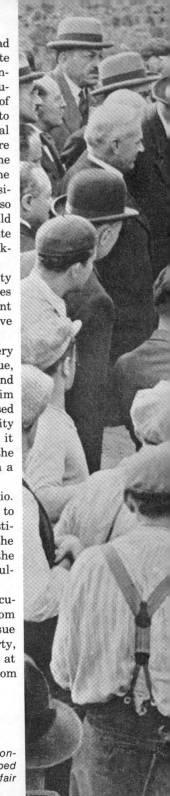

Right: Gaston Doumergue (holding the hammer), the 'non-political' politician whose accession to the premiership helped calm the Third Republic at the height of the Stavisky affair

Chapter 2

The Leagues

There were not lacking in France either men or ideas opposed to the parliamentary regime of the Third Republic. The riots of 6th February were their work, organised as they were into national organisations called Leagues, deliberately seeking a change of regime even when they lacked a clear idea of what they intended or the drive to bring it into effect. The oldest of them, the *Action Française,* began with a resurgence and refurbishing of monarchism after the Dreyfus affair in the 1890s; by 1934 it had several rivals, of which the most notable and noticeable was the *Croix de Feu.*

The man who first gave an intellectual basis to the modern authoritarian movement was Charles Maurras. He was a lonely man. He was born in 1868 at Martigues in Provence and conceived an early ambition to join the Navy. But at the age of 14 he became deaf. Already bookish, he became more so. At 17 he went to Paris and began work as a journalist – but an intellectual journalist, criticising and writing from literary sources rather than participating in human affairs. Consistently over the next sixty years he developed his critique of republican France in some 20,000 articles. His appeal lay in the uniform repetition of his ideas over a long period of time, in the comprehensive character of his critique, covering politics and literature alike, and the apparent justification which he thus gave to the ignoble emotions of xenophobia, anti-Semitism, and authoritarianism.

The values of French parliamentary democracy were precisely those which Maurras denounced under the slogan 'Reaction above all'. He condemned the Revolution and exalted the *Ancien Régime* which preceded it: the Revolution was anti-French, for it destroyed the true France of monarchy, Catholicism, and a classical inheritance. He rejected democracy, which would take power away from the elite and give it to the herd, and he rejected justice as it had been advocated in support of Dreyfus on the grounds that abstract justice was mean-

Left: The power of the Right—a joint demonstration held by the militant Camelots du Roi *and* Solidarité Française *leagues*

29

ingless, that true justice was only to be found after the proper order of the state, with its inequality corresponding to the natural inequality of men, had been established. The whole of this creed was cast in a nationalistic mould, for all the ideas which he denounced he ascribed to the pernicious influence of Jews, foreigners, *métèques* – people who were half-French. Palestine, Geneva, Germany were all variously seen as the origin of the different forms of anti-French virus.

Maurras might have remained an isolated figure at the centre of an intellectual circle had not his ideas recruited supporters far more able to act as propagandists and organisers than he was himself. Chief amongst them was Léon Daudet, son of the novelist, Alphonse Daudet. In 1908 he brought his talent and his capital to the cause of Maurras and made the newspaper *L'Action Française* into a vehicle for Maurras' ideas and his own polemical skill. Every day it was able to turn out its mixture of violent diatribe and political argument, calumny, invective, and literary criticism and so build up a clientèle of nationalists and anti-Semites, royalists, and Catholics.

The movement of the *Action Française* probably numbered about 60,000 by the 1930s; it included a militant activist group, the *Camelots du Roi*. These, together with the newspaper, brought violence and disorder into French public life. That they did may appear paradoxical, since the attraction of *Action Française* to some of its supporters was the promise it seemed to hold out of the safeguarding of traditional values, the honour of France, the maintenance of an ordered society. The paradox indeed proved too great for the established leaders of those institutions which *Action Française* claimed to support. As early as 1914 the Holy Office had placed some of the works of Maurras and the journal on the Index, but the Pope had not published the decree in the existing state of international crisis. In December 1926 his successor issued the condemnation, and included in it the daily *L'Action Française*. His action was followed by the proscriptions of the French bishops prohibiting religious marriages or burial to adherents of *Action Française*. Ten years later the royal pretender, the Duc de Guise, issued a declaration dissociating himself from the movement: 'If its political doctrine postulates the monarchical principle, the teachings of its school, on the contrary, have revealed themselves incompatible with the traditions of the House of France.'

Right: *The trophy room at the* Action Française *HQ where the banners and other souvenirs captured forcibly from the French Socialist and Communist organisations were displayed*

The Stavisky riots came between the two condemnations; they undoubtedly provided the movement with a great boost after the first. There was for the moment plenty to demonstrate about. The *Camelots du Roi* were in the forefront of the riots of 6th February. *Action Française* exploited the corruption of the parliamentarians and developed the idea that France was in the grip of a conspiracy of Radical politicians and freemasons working through the *Sûreté*. This was the national police force – bitter rivals of the police under the Paris prefecture. It was accused of responsibility for Stavisky's death, and charged, too, with the much more mysterious death, at the end of February, of Albert Prince, a judge who was found bound and drugged on the railway line near Dijon after he had promised sensational statements about the complicity of his chief, Pressard, in the Stavisky affair.

But in 1934 *Action Française* was to some extent being overtaken by the organisation which was to have the most prominence over the next two years – the *Criox de Feu*. Its part in the demonstration of 6th February was something of a sideshow on the left bank, away from the main scene of action in the Place de la Concorde, and it was accused by some of being too easily turned back by the police. But it acquired an exotic and violent appeal and achieved the appearance of dynamism in the following years.

A French *führer*?

The *Croix de Feu* began in 1927 as an organisation for distinguished ex-servicemen – those who had been cited at least once for gallantry in the field. In 1929 it became less exacting in its membership requirements, admitting those who had served six months in the trenches. In the same year it admitted into its ranks the man who was to be its leader – Colonel Casimir de la Rocque. He had established his credentials as an ex-serviceman – having served in Morocco, on the Western Front, on the staff of Marshal Foch, and in Poland. He retired in 1926 and took up a post with the *Compagnie Générale de l'Electricité*. But, for all his army experience, his ambitions for the *Croix de Feu* were political. In the absence of any other leader with equal vision as to the way the movement should go, he succeeded in taking control of it, creating a new class of members, the *Volontaires Nationaux* – who only had to feel like ex-servicemen without ever having actually served – and turning the movement to support of right-wing candidates at the elections of 1932.

Left: Bemedalled veterans of the right-wing Croix de Feu *league*

33

To that extent the *Croix de Feu* had leadership; it also had money, as a result of the inclinations of the perfume and talcum powder manufacturer François Coty. The Coty business was eminently successful in appealing to the taste of middle-class women. When any one of them — in England, Holland, or France — bought a tin of talcum powder she made a small contribution to the anti-parliamentary movement in France.

However, the *Croix de Feu* was not François Coty's favourite organisation: this was the *Solidarité Française,* founded on his initiative in 1933. Supposedly it had some 180,000 members in 1934 — three times as many as the *Croix de Feu;* but the figures are unsubstantiated and, in the case of *Solidarité Française,* particularly unreliable. Both *Croix de Feu* and *Solidarité Française* were nationalist and authoritarian. *Solidarité Française* believed in 'France for the French' — although this did not prevent it recruiting poor immigrants from North Africa, nicknamed *sidis,* so that it was dubbed by the Left the *sidilarité française.* The programme of the *Croix de Feu* included economic nationalism — making France economically self-sufficient — the strengthening of the executive, rearmament, and anti-Communism.

There were two other major organisations in these years when it was fashionable to join Leagues — both of them founded in the 1920s. The smaller of them claimed to be Fascist; its members called themselves *Francistes* and their leader Marcel Bucard paid homage to Mussolini — as well he might, since his movement received large subsidies in the 1930s through the Italian Press attaché in Paris. It had at least one of the qualities of an elitist organisation — it remained small (although not by design) and was estimated to have between twelve and fifteen hundred members. In size it was outclassed by the *Jeunesses patriotes,* founded in 1924 by Pierre Taittinger in opposition to the incompetence of Radical governments and the supposed insidious threat from the Left. It claimed 90,000 members.

The Republic in danger?
There were thus undoubtedly combustible materials in France at the beginning of 1934. The country, especially in its agricultural section, was still suffering from the effects of the slump. The rewards of having won the First World War seemed slender indeed, and were threatened by the rise of Nazism in Germany. Governments and parliaments seemed more concerned with feathering their own nests by protecting such men as Stavisky than in

Right: *July 1934 — the leader of the* Croix de Feu, *Colonel Casimir de la Rocque, harangues his followers at a Paris rally*

safeguarding the interests of the electorate. The tradition of anti-parliamentarianism was given fresh impetus by the activities of the Leagues. Did this mean that the Republic was in danger?

The answer must surely be that the greatest danger came less from the existence of the Leagues and more from the weaknesses of the parliamentary regime itself. Historians have failed to discover any concerted plan, on 6th February, for any kind of coup d'état. Yet the Chautemps government resigned because of its implication in the Stavisky affair, because of the criticisms to which it was subjected in the Chamber, and because of demonstrations in the streets — finally no doubt because it was the easiest way out. Its successor, the government of Daladier, secured a vote of confidence in the Chamber and yet abdicated its responsibility because of riots outside.

This sequence of events at once demonstrated and aggravated the weakness of the Radical Party. More than anything else the Radicals stood for the defence of the Republic; but in a moment of crisis they abandoned power, declined the offer of Blum to hold on to office, were divided amongst themselves and discredited by their part in the Stavisky scandal.

The values which the Radical Party claimed to stand for — democracy, liberty, secularism, social progress — provided themes which could be phrased in appropriate oratory in such a way as to guarantee a harmonious glow at a party meeting and produce rounds of applause. But their application was centred increasingly in the parliamentary sphere and given parliamentary interpretation. All too easily democracy was interpreted as the freedom to make parliamentary combinations; the Republic was identified with the mode of life of a deputy, and secularism became a guide to parliamentary alliances.

The preoccupation with parliamentary politics for its own sake brought a predictable reward. When the system was shaken from the outside the Radicals scarcely knew how to act. Their resignations in 1934 dislocated the political system and they did not return to the full exercise of power until April 1938. By that time parliamentary life was virtually at a standstill.

Nor did the Socialist Party, which, in an electoral alliance in 1932, had ensured the success of the Left, provide any better support for parliamentary government. It too believed in the transformation of society. It was unwilling to assume power until it could lead the

Maurice Utrillo

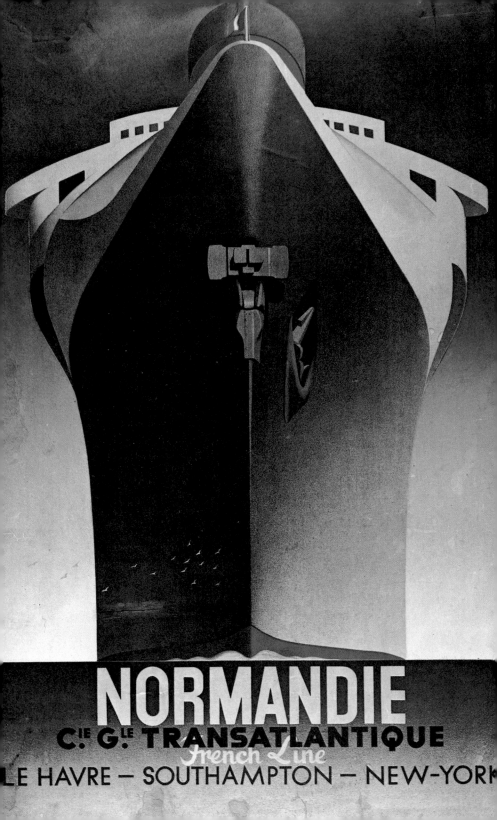

NORMANDIE
Cie Gle TRANSATLANTIQUE
French Line
LE HAVRE — SOUTHAMPTON — NEW-YORK

government, intent on the reform of society until it secured a majority. But in practice this all too easily degenerated into disputes within the party about tactics to be followed, alliances to be made, points of ideology to be substantiated.

Even more important was the fact that the internal problems of France in these years were primarily economic. The level of economic discussion was even lower in France than in the United States of America. As an academic subject economics was generally studied in the Faculty of Law; there were no serious journals of economics nor writers to carry on the tradition of Say, Gide, and Rist or to compete with the English and Americans.

The combination of the structure of politics and the ignorance of economics made it that much easier for different sections of the country to blame each other. The Left won electoral victories, then saw the government collapse and, without a general election, its replacement by a right-wing government supported by a different majority in the same Chamber. Working people found their own economic situation in the same plight as that of the country, and would readily place the blame on a conspiracy of '200 families' or a 'wall of money'. The Right for their part attributed economic weakness to the demands of labour, and saw themselves excluded from power by the game of parliamentary politics. They had always been prone to believe that instead of being governed they were manipulated by a series of conspiracies. For decades they had attacked the order of freemasons, which did indeed have an extensive membership and which facilitated political contacts and arrangements, especially amongst Radical politicians. To this traditional target of attack were now added the Communists, whom the Right did not always distinguish clearly from anyone else on the Left. It was in this way that the most nationalist of nations ceased to be able to recognise itself and divided in an atmosphere of mutual recrimination.

Chapter 3

Barthou
and theYear of Laval

In 1934, the second year of Hitler's rule, the international problems created by the existence of his Nazi state in the centre of Europe proved to be a continuation of those which had concerned British and French statesmen since Versailles. Two questions predominated: the question of rearmament and the question of Austria.

The Versailles settlement left a major problem in the field of armaments by completely disarming Germany while expressing a vague commitment on the part of the victors to disarm as well. Through the 1920s British and French negotiators had disagreed on the possibilities of disarmament, to which the British attached far greater importance than the French as a means to security. But their differences of opinion were further complicated by the rising German demand to rearm to a position of 'equality' with the other European powers. The Weimar governments always cheated to a limited extent on the disarmament clauses of the Versailles settlement. But at the same time the Germans pursued a policy of 'fulfilment' of the treaty, accepting the western frontiers of Germany as permanent, signing the Locarno Treaty, agreeing to the Dawes Plan for reparations and, while not accepting the permanence of the eastern frontiers, agreeing that they should not be changed by force.

In these circumstances Britain and France had the choice between a tough attitude towards German rearmament, on the grounds that Germany had shown bad faith and could not be trusted with any armaments, and a more conciliatory posture based on the assumption that if Germany freely signed an arms agreement it would be kept and would permit British and French disarmament. No clear-cut choice between these alternatives was made. But Weimar Germany withdrew from the world disarmament conference in July 1932 and was persuaded to return (in December) by a formula recognising Germany's equality of rights in a system providing security for all. The next month Hitler became Chancellor.

Left: Foreign affairs minister Louis Barthou (right) and King Alexander of Yugoslavia drive through Marseilles, October 1934

His tactics on first coming to power did not help to clarify the minds of the British and French (nor were they intended to). They were a repetition of those which had brought him to power by legal means in Germany even as he broke the bonds of the Versailles Treaty he proposed fresh arrangements for the maintenance of peace. The British reaction to this policy was relatively favourable. The French government took a different course. It decided that it was not worth continuing with disarmament negotiations, and that instead it must make provision for its own defence. In a note of 17th April 1934 it withdrew from any further efforts to achieve disarmament by agreement and announced that henceforth it would safeguard its security 'by its own means'.

The practical difference which this made was slight. The logic of the note was that rearmament should be put in hand; in the event it was first delayed by policies of economy and deflation and then hindered by the weaknesses of the French industrial base and the need for social reform. Failing to produce concrete results, it nonetheless had an adverse political effect to the extent that it added to the conflict of views between Britain and France.

This was the more to be regretted since the movement to the Right had brought into office, in Doumergue's Cabinet, one of the most talented men who conducted French foreign affairs between the wars. Louis Barthou belonged to an old generation of Republicans, conservative in most things except in their attitude to the basic concepts of republicanism. Barthou was elected deputy in the Basses Pyrénées in 1889 and was a minister by the time he was thirty. A superb orator in the style of the French Chamber he was thus influential enough for his commitment to the cause of Dreyfus to be of major importance in the development of the Affair. He had held most of the more important ministries – Public Works, Interior, War, Public Instruction – and since 1931 had been the leading member of the Senate Committee on Foreign Affairs.

Back in office at the age of seventy-two he took a traditional view of the German danger and the possible means to counter it. France should rearm, and should establish a ring of alliances encircling Germany.

At the same time the material from which such alliances could be made was changing. The Soviet Union, it appeared, was returning to a policy of defence against Germany. The period of the 1920s when Germany and

Left: The assassination of Alexander and Barthou – having fired into the royal car, the assassin is held by the chauffeur while a mounted cavalryman strikes out at him with a sabre

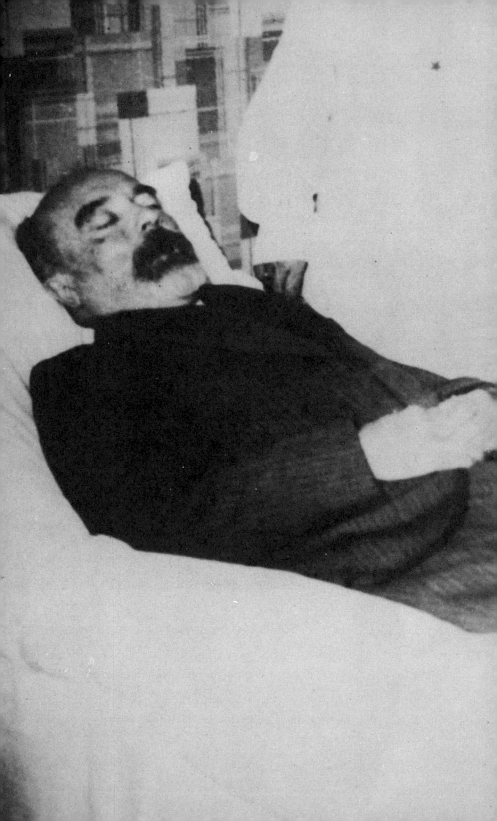

Russia formed an entente of common interest as the outcasts of Europe was past. In 1934 the Soviet Union joined the League of Nations, which previously it had denounced as merely an alliance of the capitalist victors, and advocated a policy of collective security. At the same time Poland, whose cause France had espoused against both Germany and Russia alike in the 1920s, now moved closer to Germany and signed a non-aggression pact with Hitler's government in January 1934.

In the east the Soviet Union thus became a potential ally. In the south the differences which had existed between France and Italy disappeared in their common concern over the independence of Austria. This independence was guaranteed, as far as Germany was concerned, by the Versailles Treaty, which forbade *Anschluss,* or union between Germany and Austria. This did not prevent many Austrians, especially the Social Democrats, from hoping that such union could be achieved, as long as the Weimar Republic survived. In 1931 a proposal was floated for a customs union between the two countries. French diplomacy, backed by financial strength, was decisive in thwarting the plan; and the Italian government joined in protesting against it. On the basis of this common interest the rivalry in the Balkans which had impaired Franco-Italian relations in the 1920s was put aside, and an agreement was reached over Tunisia, which, under French rule, had a large Italian population.

With Hitler's accession to power the shape of a possible union between Germany and Austria was changed. The prospect was no longer attractive to Austrian Social Democrats. In any case the autocratic Chancellor of Austria, Dollfuss, carried out a brutal suppression of the Social Democratic Party in 1933. *Anschluss* now became a Nazi cause. Impatient for success the Austrian Nazis won Hitler's approval for a *putsch* which they carried out in July 1934. Dollfuss was assassinated—ironically he became the first victim of the Nazis, after his own bombardment of workers' flats in Vienna in 1933 had done more than anything else to alert European labour movements to the dangers of Fascism. The coup failed; but it brought Italian troops to the Brenner, who, since they were on manoeuvres, may not have realised that they were participating in a great diplomatic event—Mussolini taking a stand against Hitler.

To that extent an alliance was established between France and Italy in common opposition to Germany. To the east Barthou's diplomacy was less successful. The plan he proposed took the form of an 'eastern Locarno'

Left: Barthou's body—the end of a vigorous foreign policy

—a system of guarantees in which Germany would participate, similar to those which guaranteed the western frontier. The weakness of the plan was that in the pursuit of a political cover for a system of security the main object almost disappeared from view. Nor did the political cover work. The British government had continuously resisted any commitment in Eastern Europe, ever since Versailles. Hitler declined to be drawn. Poland, standing fast on its new policy of a bilateral agreement with Germany, would not join a security system with Russia or with Czechoslovakia, with which it nurtured a dispute over the small area of Teschen.

A single advantage was secured which, in other circumstances, might have been of crucial importance—Barthou established the basis of an alliance with the Soviet Union, thus renewing, potentially, the alliance of 1893. But he did not live to sign it.

The death of Barthou

On 9th October 1934 he was riding in a motor car with King Alexander of Yugoslavia in Marseilles. They had enjoyed an official lunch together and had presumably been discussing the implications for Franco-Yugoslav relations of the new French rapprochement with Italy. But for one man in the crowd it was more important that Alexander was a Serb king against whom a group of Croat terrorists had taken up arms. He had no difficulty in breaking through the inadequate guards and discharging his revolver into the car.

Alexander, the target of his attack, was killed. Barthou and General Georges (who was to be second in command to Gamelin when war broke out in 1939) were both wounded. Barthou calmly stepped from the car without assistance, but was bleeding more heavily than a man of seventy-two could easily sustain. Interest was concentrated on the King—a more important personage, even when dead, than a minister—until at last Barthou was conveyed in a motor car along the bumpy *pavé* of the Canebière to hospital. He was then given a transfusion, but it came too late to save his life.

He was succeeded at the Foreign Ministry by Laval, who made a show of continuing the foreign policy which Barthou had inaugurated and signed the alliance with Russia. But in fact a period of firmness towards Germany had come to an end. Whether it would have continued had Barthou survived is doubtful, given the instability of French government and the forces making for appeasement; however that may be, Laval's view of

Left: *The trial of Zvonim Popicil (left) and Ivan Bagic who were accomplices in the assassination of the Yugoslav king*

both Russia and Germany was totally different from that of his predecessor.

The year 1934 had ended badly for France. The semi-fascist Leagues had failed to overthrow the Republic, but the government had lost itself in the irrelevancy of a dispute over the powers of the Premier. It had neither dissolved the Leagues nor solved the economic problem from which they gained much of their strength.

The basis of an alliance had been laid with Italy. But Mussolini took pride in having been a model for Hitler and was bent on a policy of grandeur for Italy. In the long run France would find it hard to offer him sufficient reward for a policy of co-operation against Hitler, when Hitler could offer the prospect of glory on his coat tails. An understanding had been reached with the Soviet Union in which there was perhaps more community of interest. But the two powers which in the long term had most in common — France and Britain — were further apart as a result of their differences over disarmament and the British refusal to see the importance of Eastern Europe.

The problems which beset France in 1935 called for a statesman of vision and courage; the parliamentary system produced instead Pierre Laval. Political renewal there was; but in this crucial year it was going on outside the Chamber, in negotiations and discussions, constructive associations between political parties and within the trade union movement, celebrated and cemented by exciting political demonstrations — which had no effect on the immediate course of governmental action.

The recession of the economy continued. It showed itself in falling production and rising unemployment, together with the export of capital. As the level of economic activity was reduced so was the return from taxation. Any attempt to balance the budget — and this was the constant ambition of successive ministers of finance — meant further economies. Such economies were made in defence and public works. But those which were felt most were the cuts in pensions and civil servants' pay.

There can be no doubt, in retrospect, about the cause of France's economic problem. The French franc was over-valued in terms of other currencies. The other major currencies — the pound sterling and the dollar — were devalued (in terms of gold) after the slump. The Belgian franc followed suit in 1935. As a result French prices remained high in relation to world prices, making it easy for foreign enterprises to compete in France while it was extremely difficult for French firms to export.

Left: Low cartoon jibes at the notorious instability of France's financial system and the insatiable greed of French financiers

Amongst French politicians Paul Reynaud – a maverick who espoused unpopular causes but was eventually proved right (and who was premier briefly in 1940) – advocated devaluation. It was rejected by the government and by the economic and political directors of the country. Lamentably weak in their knowledge of economics they were particularly myopic on this question. Defensive in their nationalism they wanted to think of France as a country sufficient to itself, independent of foreign trade. With a peasant-like attachment to the soil they thought of their country as a garden which could produce all that was required for its own needs. And they thought that to 'save the franc' was the same as saving France.

With devaluation ruled out the only other way to reduce prices – and to economise on the government budget – was by deflation, and this was the course that was followed, both by Pierre Flandin, premier from November 1934 to June 1935, and later by Laval.

The effects were paradoxical. In the short run it did not make the industrial worker or even the civil servant worse off (as long as they were working). The fall in money wages was more than compensated by the fall in prices, so that real wages rose. But the long-term effect was to reduce the level of economic activity and so to deprive the country of potential production. Meanwhile the amount of money coming into a family fell – and this was far more important in affecting political attitudes than the rise in real wages.

The political implications were important too – and demonstrate how far the action of the government moved away from popular politics. The deputies had no incentive to vote deflationary policies. In consequence they were legislated by a system of decree laws which obviated the need for parliament to carry the obloquy of an unpopular policy. Moreover, the deflationary policy was continued through 1935 into the period of the electoral campaign of 1936. There was no attempt to introduce a more popular policy for electoral reasons, less because of the government's commitment to saving the franc than because the government was remote from the people.

Deflation also meant economies in military spending. The total expenditure on armaments was overtaken by the size of German expenditure. A massive proportion of the military budget went on building and maintaining the Maginot Line. The defensiveness of the Maginot Line mentality was thereby enhanced. Soldiers and civilians were discouraged from even thinking of new and modern equipment for which appropriation might not be

Right: *1935 – Premier Pierre Laval holds a press conference*

forthcoming. This led to the postponement of military manoeuvres in an attempt to save money.

The effect of these economies became evident in 1940. Meanwhile the psychological effect of deflation was to reinforce the division in French society. Socialists, Left-wing Radicals, and Communists campaigned against the government's policies. The Socialist newspaper *Le Populaire* wrote in July 1935: 'The deflationary measures constitute a real provocation for all workers in the public services, pensioners, and small producers; they are a real attempt against the Nation.'

Others blamed not the Right but politicians in general, and gave their support to authoritarianism. The division in society was moreover enhanced by the continuing activities of the Leagues. They were now no nearer to taking power—Colonel de la Rocque repeatedly talked of their doing so when the moment was opportune, but that moment never came. Their activity consisted of meetings, marches, and demonstrations, organised with military efficiency and military discipline—a quality which made them attractive to many of the participants. At the most spectacular of these demonstrations, in Algiers, they were able to put on a show with some thirty aeroplanes. Other meetings, often held on the estate of some wealthy notable, were made prominent by the deployment of fast cars and the patrolling of the roads by *Croix de Feu* men.

Towards the Popular Front

Spectacular as these activities were, their effect was not in bringing the Leagues to power, but in producing a response from the Left, facilitating the movement towards the Popular Front. Reaction against the Leagues and the change of policy of the French Communist Party over the instructions which Laval brought back from Moscow made possible the great *quatorze juillet* of the Popular Front in 1935 when, to the sound of the *Marseillaise* mingling with the *Internationale,* the Left reclaimed Joan of Arc from the Right, taking her as a symbol of a nation of the Left—as *fille du peuple*.

But while decisive events were thus in formation at home, Laval was engaged in the conduct of a foreign policy which left France in a markedly worse international position than when he took office. It must be said that Laval was ill-suited to the task. He was a man who had risen from humble origins by dint of hard work and perseverance; but he had developed neither intellectual power nor any great historical vision or sense of purpose for the future. In certain circumstances his talents were those which won victories: he was tenacious, patient in holding on through tough negotiations to get

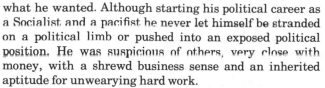

what he wanted. Although starting his political career as a Socialist and a pacifist he never let himself be stranded on a political limb or pushed into an exposed political position. He was suspicious of others, very close with money, with a shrewd business sense and an inherited aptitude for unwearying hard work.

Perhaps these qualities came from his native background. He grew up in Châteldon in the north of Auvergne —far from the sea, far from the frontiers of France. His father was a butcher who also kept the village café. He left school at the age of twelve, but continued to educate himself, with encouragement from the dignitaries of the village. He became a lawyer and then, in May 1914, a Socialist deputy for the working-class Paris constituency of Aubervilliers—of which he also became Mayor until he was deprived of his office by decree after the liberation of France in 1944. His army service, before 1914, was brief. It was terminated by his being unfit with varicose veins; he did not travel until he did so as leader of his government. He had a deep and passionate attachment to his origins—the land, the cultivation of vines (which he continued to supervise until his trial in 1945), the ordinary people of his region. At the same time he enriched himself by the purchase of two newspapers (*Le Moniteur de Puy-de-Dome,* which he ran successfully, and the *Républicain de Lyon,* which he sold at a profit), a printing works, and Radio-Lyon.

His political success came from the suitability of his own talents to the parliamentary system of the Third Republic. He was not a party man, nor an ideologist— he could pick up support from a wide range of political contacts with whom he could establish something in common without having to invoke party loyalty or dedication to an ideal. This gave him political influence, which he strengthened by his indefatigable tenacity. But the qualities which brought success in the special world of Third Republic politics were not adapted to international politics, let alone to the threatening world of the dictators.

The situation which he inherited from Barthou was one which offered two possible alliances—with Russia and with Italy. The entente with Britain was a weak and uncertain factor. One of these alliances, that with Russia, Laval converted into a formal treaty, signed in Paris in May 1935. He immediately followed its signature with a visit to Moscow, from which he won a considerable political victory—Stalin agreed that the French Communists

Left: Pressure from the militant Left continues—Paris demonstration by the ARAC organisation (left-wing combat veterans)

55

should cease their opposition to French rearmament. Laval was able to return to Paris as the 'realist' who accepted the subordination of French Communists to Moscow and used it to his advantage and the advantage of France.

But the French commitment to the Russian alliance was unreal in its international aspect and harmful in its domestic implications. Laval's view of alliances was not that they should act as a deterrent in the cut-throat world of international relations, far less that they were the prelude to a combination of forces in war—the very idea of which he pushed from his mind. The purpose of an alliance was to strengthen his hand in negotiation with Germany. Indeed his lack of enthusiasm for the connection with Russia would probably have prevented the completion of Barthou's work, were it not for Hitler's provocative announcement of Germany's intended rearmament (including the introduction of conscription) in March 1935.

In consequence the French public welcomed the alliance. The Right saw it as a renewal of the traditional Franco-Russian alliance. But in the course of the next year it acquired a different aspect. As a deterrent to Germany in lacked credibility. The Russian government wanted to supplement the alliance with staff talks. But neither Laval nor his successors were prepared to enter such talks—at first through simple suspicion of the Soviet Union, then (when Blum was premier) through anxiety about Soviet security at a time when leading Russian generals were being accused in state trials of being in contact with the Germans. There were practical difficulties, too, in the implementation of the alliance, given that Poland and Rumania stood between Russia and Germany.

In any case Hitler was not deterred by the alliance. On the contrary he was aware of the strength of hostility to Communism amongst the conservatives of Britain and France and, with characteristic adroitness, argued that the Franco-Soviet pact invalidated the Locarno Treaty guaranteeing the western frontier of Germany — and confirming the demilitarisation of the Rhineland. By playing this line he could reasonably hope that the alliance would be abandoned in favour of Locarno, or that both would be dropped together. In fact he was even more favoured than that. Within France the alliance be-

*Right: German cartoon reproves Popular Front France for submitting to the clasp of the Russian bear. **Next page:** French magazine illustration of an anti-French school text allegedly distributed by the Nazi regime. **Page 60:** Sly French cartoon suggests that the only practical result of the three-power Stresa conference was to encourage Italy's tourist industry*

Nr. 20 – 89. Jahrg.
Berlin, 17. Mai 1936

Preis 52

Kladderadatsch

Was ist paradog?

Der Franzose befiehlt:

Du bist allein schuld am Krieg, musst Land hergeben;

u. alle Kolonien

Du mußt alles bezahlen,
" " liefern tag u. Nacht Züge voll Gold, Holz, Kohle, Farbe, Eisen, Kupfer,

Gold | Kupfer | Eisen | Holz | Kohle | Farbe

Du mußt aufbauen alle zerschossenen Häuser u. Städte,
" " abgeben alle Schiffe, Luftschiffe, Festungen, Waffen, Soldaten.

Du mußt untergehen u. sterben

Der Franzose sagt:

Erzberger   unterschrieb. „Die Hände sollen verdorren, die diesen Frieden untersch...

Gute Menschen weinen.

Hitler weint.

„Nun aber konnte ich nicht anders, es ist alles um-

sonst gewesen, umsonst der Hunger u. Durst,
" die Todesangst
" der Tod von 200000 "
(Mein Kampf

Wir sind Knechte von Frankreich geworden.

Fr.

DEUTSCHLAND-
FIEBERT

-München soll Moskau werden-

Kirchenglocken
läuten Tag u. Nacht -
Türm - Häuser - zer-
schossen.

Hilfe suchen
Hungerzüge u. große
Vater Klowo

spartakisten erschießen
die Leute in den Anlagen; Geiseln

er Jude Eisner sagt: Weg mit Vaterland! Weg mit Gott! Weg mit den
Eltern! Weg mit den Führern! Nieder mit dem 8 St.-Tag!

lles fürchtet sich: Graf Arko knallt Eisner nieder /: 24.2.1919:/ Epp befreit mit
Freikorps Wolf u. Werdenfels München — Alles dankt Gott.

ie Reichswehr wird gegründet.

e cri de par

HEBDOMADAIRE ILLUSTRÉ
Directeur - Rédacteur en Chef : Paul DOLLFUS

Paris-VIII°
AC 58-95 —

Vendredi 19
Reg. du Commerce

RESULTATS PRATIQUES DE STRESA ? ? ?

came increasingly a bogey of the Right, and the growing strength of the Popular Front deepened still further the gulf in French society as the Right saw themselves in danger of being governed by Socialists and Communists in alliance with the Soviet Union.

Meanwhile, Laval continued his task of 'organising peace'. His policy was to yield to Germany where French interests were not affected, and to try to strengthen his hand for negotiation where they were. To that extent it involved from the start a diminution of France's claim to be a European great power, for the very definition of that status meant that French interests were co-extensive with the European international system; it also supposed that Hitler would conduct his foreign policy in accordance with Laval's rules of the game—even though there was no evidence, in the way Hitler had acquired and consolidated power in Germany, that this would be so.

Nonetheless, it must be said that Laval's first concession to Germany was the more dramatic in part because of the unrealistic stance of Louis Barthou. This was over the question of the Saar territory. The Treaty of Versailles had placed the Saar under League of Nations control, with provision for a plebiscite to be held fifteen years later. As the date of the plebiscite drew near Barthou did his best to influence the Saarlanders towards France. He followed the tradition of French governments which, after the First World War, tried to set up a separatist Rhineland republic. When the plebiscite took place, on 13th January 1935, more than 90 per cent voted for reunion with Germany. It seems inconceivable therefore that the Saarlanders could have been persuaded to prefer France to Germany.

But it was in Hitler's interest to make the most of what would in any case be a political success for him and he employed typical Nazi methods of intrigue and determination to bring this about. Barthou replied by financing anti-German propaganda and by threatening to send French troops to maintain order. Replacing Barthou, Laval immediately reversed his policy and offered reassurance to Germany. But while Barthou's policy would have invited diplomatic defeat for France, that of Laval was rightly interpreted as one of pandering to Hitler, and won neither respect nor restraint from him in return.

The Saarland is in the heart of industrial Europe. As the Saarlanders prepared to vote, other events were in progress on the barren and uninviting frontier between Italian Somaliland, on the East African coast, and Ethiopia.

Chapter 4
Ethiopia
and the Rhineland

Mussolini's expansionist ambitions proved disastrous for the future of Europe. They did no good to Italy, which moved a step further towards dependence on Germany; they sabotaged the League of Nations; they set the example for German aggression; they added still further to the divisions within France.

The fact remains that as 1934 ended Mussolini had two objectives: to attack Ethiopia and to join in restraint of German power. Britain and France shared the second objective with Italy; they had to decide what should be their reaction to Mussolini's expansionism. To allow the conquest of Ethiopia by Italy – quite apart from considerations of morality – was not possible in the simple manner of 19th-century *realpolitik*. Both countries were members of the League of Nations and the Italian attack brought into question both the institutions of collective security and the willingness of the other powers to resist unprovoked attack, regardless of whether their immediate interests were at stake.

These considerations were of no importance to Laval. He had inherited from his predecessor the understanding with Italy over the independence of Austria. He succeeded in turning the international protest about the murder of King Alexander and Louis Barthou against Hungary (where the Croat terrorists had their camp) rather than Italy (which had also supported them). More important, in January 1935 he visited Mussolini in Rome and signed a series of agreements – the Rome agreements – settling minor frontier differences between the Italian and French empires and questions of citizenship in Tunisia. This was the uppermost, public layer of the agreements. Next came a secret protocol on disarmament with reference to Germany and an exchange of letters on French economic interests in Ethiopia, relating to the traffic of the Djibouti-Addis Ababa railway. Deepest of all was a verbal understanding which Laval gave to Mussolini that he could have a free hand in Ethiopia.

Left: Punch *cartoon of October 1935 shows Laval, 'the animal trainer', attempting to control Mussolini's aggressive Italy*

63

Two months later, in March, Hitler announced his decision to embark on rearmament—including conscription. His provocative declaration brought a verbal riposte from France, Italy, and Britain. Laval, Mussolini, and the British Foreign Secretary Sir John Simon met at Stresa and produced a declaration stating their opposition to 'any unilateral repudiation of treaties which may endanger the peace of Europe'. In appearance a concerted stand had been taken against Germany—the appearance was sufficiently convincing for the term 'Stresa front' to become current. Hitler, however, judged it for what it was, and saw no danger of actual resistance being offered to the rearmament of Germany.

For Mussolini the front was a facade which concealed something of more immediate importance. He believed that the declaration confirmed the verbal agreement he had reached with Laval in Rome, and that the Stresa declaration's reference to 'Europe' implied that he had a free hand in Ethiopia. It was indeed Laval's intention that this should be so. But Mussolini's campaign against Ethiopia was a long drawn-out affair and as the year proceeded Laval found an ever-increasing part of his political skill being devoted to treading the tight-rope he had chosen for himself.

The incident which was to serve Mussolini as pretext for his conquest had occurred at the beginning of December 1934, when some thirty native troops in the Italian army were killed on the frontier of Eritrea and Ethiopia —in Ethiopian territory which had been under Italian control since 1928. The Ethiopian government sought arbitration, then took the question to the League of Nations (to which France had originally sponsored its membership). Up to a point Mussolini was prepared to accept diplomatic discussion since it gave him time to establish his army ready for attack—carrying it in boats through the Suez Canal. But the delay and the debate in the League made it possible for the supporters of collective security to mobilise the small powers, British public opinion, and, to a much less significant degree, the Left in France.

Nor did Laval find any comfort in the policy of the British government, which was indeed in total disarray. Although the government had joined the Stresa front to protest against German rearmament it had not abandoned the optimistic hope that a treaty could be signed with Germany which would be better than allowing Germany to rearm without restriction. This was a policy with which Laval had much sympathy—far more so than Barthou. He joined with the British in discussions of an

Right: Parisians study a map showing the events in Ethiopia

64

'air pact' to limit the air forces of Britain, France, and Germany. Then, suddenly, without effective consultation with France the British recognised and accepted German naval rearmament by signing an Anglo-German naval agreement. On paper it satisfied the Admiralty's needs by restricting German building of surface warships. But in practice it had no effect on German naval construction, while its political effect was considerable. It discredited the Stresa front, made nonsense of resistance to German rearmament, and greatly damaged Anglo-French relations.

The inconsistencies of British policy towards Italy went even further. It pursued three policies at the same time. First, it responded to a surge of public opinion in favour of the League and Ethiopia. It fought an election on its support for collective security, and at the meeting of the League in September British Foreign Secretary Samuel Hoare made a speech which convinced his audience that Britain would lead collective action against Italy. The momentum towards sanctions was greatly strengthened. But at the same time it tried to devise a plan of concessions which would satisfy Mussolini while stopping short of the conquest of Ethiopia. And finally it prepared for war lest some rash action by Italy should precipitate an unintended conflict.

Laval's path, although its immediate objective was clear-cut, became the more difficult to tread. Although he had no reason to trust the British government (and trust was not an attitude which came naturally to him) he had the assurance of Hoare that it was not his government's intention to impose sanctions to the point of risking war with Italy. Possibly he would have felt more secure had he guessed the interpretation which the British government gave to collective security – namely, that they would only act as part of a genuinely collective action, for which an essential condition was French participation.

But when Mussolini's army and air force launched a full-scale attack against Ethiopia in October 1935 Laval had no alternative but to comply in the imposition of sanctions against Italy. The sanctions were inadequate to restrain Italy – they did not include oil, while supplies of coal and other essentials reached Italy from Germany. But for a time they seemed to be effective – because the Italian army proved so inadequate in the field that people could attribute its reverses to sanctions. When the Italians resorted to the use of poison gas the sense of moral outrage only strengthened further the demand for effective sanctions.

A combination of political problems made Laval's position precarious – indeed it is a measure of the in-

effectiveness to which the Radical Party had been reduced by the events of February 1934 that he was able to survive. He was attacked for his deflationary measures, and he was accused of conniving in the activity of the Leagues. He had the strong support of the Right, who saw much virtue in Mussolini and none in the League of Nations; but the Communists were pressing for the immediate formation of a Popular Front and the Left of the Radical Party criticised its leadership for affording the Cabinet the support on which its majority depended.

The Hoare-Laval Plan

It was in these circumstances that Samuel Hoare met Laval in Paris to agree on a plan which would be presented to Mussolini. The plan was not a new departure in British policy—merely a new instalment of one of three conflicting strands, though the one which had been least in public view. Without regard to the rights of Ethiopia it proposed the cession of territory and the award of economic rights to Italy, with provision for an Ethiopian outlet to the sea.

The agreement immediately became public knowledge—an official communiqué was published stating that agreement had been reached, and the plan itself was leaked to the Press. The outcry in Britain killed the plan and brought the resignation of the Foreign Secretary; a month later a similar, though delayed, reaction in France brought the resignation of Laval.

The Hoare-Laval plan was killed. It probably came too late to offer Mussolini any incentive to stop short of military victory, but there was no possibility of his accepting it once it was a public document. In the early spring the French government, under pressure from the British, returned to a policy of sanctions. But they were still incomplete and ineffective. In March 1936 the Emperor of Ethiopia was forced to accept defeat.

The effect of the Ethiopian war was to precipitate the alliance between Germany and Italy. France not only ceased to have an ally in Italy, it did not have diplomatic representation until, in 1938, the Daladier government agreed to accredit an ambassador to 'the King of Italy and Emperor of Ethiopia'—it did so, still, in the hope of reaching Hitler through Mussolini. The war also destroyed the League of Nations as an effective institution—not beyond repair, but sufficiently to justify the sceptics who had poured scorn on its value in international politics. For France, dependent on others for the maintenance of its security against Germany, the blow was severe.

Left: Pierre Laval at Stresa in 1935 where France, Italy, Britain sought a common front against Hitler's territorial ambitions

There was another serious casualty: the relationship between Great Britain and France. Laval and his supporters attributed the defeat of his policy of peace with Germany to the perfidy of the British. Later, they justified their collaboration with Germany in the government of Vichy in these terms.

British distrust of France was no less. One member of the British Cabinet was intent, when the crisis opened, on a firm stand and maintenance of the League, but he found that Laval 'jibbed' and 'wriggled' and that 'the French have been as disloyal as they could'. This was Neville Chamberlain. His distrust of France was to be of crucial importance in the crisis over Czechoslovakia.

The fall of Laval's government in January 1936 and the failure of his Ethiopian policy left France very vulnerable. The full extent of its vulnerability Hitler was best able to judge.

Pierre Laval's resignation was followed by prolonged negotiations which ultimately led to the formation of a government headed by Albert Sarraut. He was an ideal person to head a caretaker government. Previously, he had been Governor-General of Indo-China. He and his brother Maurice were closely associated with *La Dépêche de Toulouse* — the most important of the provincial Radical Party dailies. He was a moderate Radical; he was known to enjoy a gay life and was the object of numerous anecdotes. He was not likely to offend anyone and it was not in his nature to take a strong stand.

Outside parliament the Right was in full hue and cry against those who, they believed, were responsible for the alienation of Italy. They had no quarrel with Italy. There was much that they admired, much that many would have imitated in Mussolini's Fascist government. They saw no reason to oppose Mussolini's claims on Ethiopia, and they had never admired the League of Nations or the system of collective security which it represented.

In *L'Action Française* Jacques Delebecque wrote of Italy: 'Delicate souls are sometimes shocked by the violence that accompanies this immense operation of national revival . . . Too bad for delicate souls! . . . there's not much room left for them in the harsh world of today. . . . The nobility of the end justifies the means that Fascism uses to achieve it.' The scathing pen of Léon Daudet asked: 'Is the Salivary Society, alias the League of Nations, going to drag us into a European Masonic war?'

The objects of the right-wing attack — the Radical Party and the Socialists — were not as determined in their opposition to Laval's policy as these attacks might suggest. The Socialists stood for collective security and disarmament; but as elections approached it was avoidance of war which came first. The Radicals were divided:

Edouard Herriot, who was the principal object of the attack, was a supporter of the Ethiopian case as well as being a Russophile, and it was his resignation which precipitated Laval's resignation. But Daladier, in spite of his advocacy of the Popular Front, apparently approved Laval's policy and certainly lacked the vision which Herriot showed in basing his case on arguments of legality and humanity.

The attack which the Right made on the Radicals provided a cover for the fact that they were at the same time abandoning their traditional attitude towards Germany. The welcome which they gave to the Franco-Soviet alliance when it was signed by Laval evaporated with the the approach of a Popular Front government. In May 1935 the pact was compared to the alliance which Francis I had made with the Turks and Richelieu had made with the German Protestants – in short it was an alliance which provided for France's security without regard to ideological considerations. But as the French Communists came to support rearmament and pressed for a League of Nations policy, as the Popular Front alliance began to have reality, the Franco-Soviet pact took on a different guise as an alliance between Russian and French Communists. Thus, while the parties of the Left were brought into association with each other through their fear of Fascism as represented by the Leagues, so the Right came to be afraid of Communism, and to see a greater danger from the French Left than from Hitler's Germany. Their real fear was that France would be dragged into a war in Eastern Europe, one fought for 'les beaux yeux de M. Staline et de M. Litvinov [Russian Foreign Minister]' and that in such a war Communism would be the only real victor.

Hitler moves

Adolf Hitler made an accurate assessment of the political disarray of France. His generals opposed his plans for the remilitarisation of the Rhineland on the grounds that their army was too weak in relation to the French. Hitler's confidence in his own judgment was based on his assessment of French politics. But he would have been equally justified had his calculation followed from purely military considerations.

The demilitarised zone of the Rhineland was all that was left in 1936 of the military guarantees vis-à-vis Germany on which the French had insisted at Versailles. Demilitarisation had been intended to serve a double purpose: to protect France from German attack, and to make it easy for French troops to cross the Rhine and

Left: Prime Minister Ramsay MacDonald arrives at Stresa

69

invade Germany. In this way the whole treaty settlement of Europe could be guaranteed. If the war were to be renewed, it would be fought on German soil, not French. If Germany were to threaten the eastern settlement, French aid could be provided for the new states of Poland or Czechoslovakia by an attack across the Rhine into Germany. This was not, perhaps, the German view of the demilitarised Rhineland. Nonetheless, the Weimar government had, in 1925, accepted the Rhineland settlement. The demilitarisation was not a residue of the Versailles *diktat*; it had been made part of the Locarno Treaty, freely signed by Germany, and guaranteed by Britain and Italy as well as Belgium, France, and Germany.

The demilitarised zone might seem therefore indispensable to French security, a keystone in the European policy of France, a testing ground for Hitler's intentions. Yet when German troops entered the Rhineland on 7th March 1936 they did so unopposed. The anxieties of Hitler's generals — whom he had been obliged to appease by a promise (probably empty) that he would withdraw if he encountered resistance — had proved groundless.

Not only that but the decision against action had, in a sense, been taken long before the French cabinet met on 7th March. The implications for French military and strategic policy of the demilitarised zone, and the foreign policy which went with it, had been easy to accept in the early 1920s when Germany was prostrate and France retained its army. By the time it was necessary to take these implications seriously, they had been abandoned. At least since the end of the 1920s military policy was defensive; in 1936 the Maginot Line, that network of concrete fortifications intended to replace the trenches (and avoid the casualties) of the First World War, was nearing completion. French strategy, as was evident three years later, was to await attack in defensive positions; and on this assumption the demilitarised section of German territory along the Rhine was of no advantage — there were no armoured brigades that were going to penetrate into it. By the same token there was no mobile force available on 7th March to counter the movement of German troops. Military reaction, insofar as it was considered at all, would have meant virtually complete mobilisation, followed by a slow, essentially defensive movement forward in open country.

Nor was remilitarisation a sudden, unforeseen event which took the French government entirely by surprise. On 12th February the War Minister, General Maurin, wrote to Flandin, the Foreign Minister, that he expected

Right: *The remilitarisation of the Rhineland — German troops march past the great cathedral of Cologne on 7th March 1936*

the question of the Rhineland to be raised by Germany
when circumstances were favourable. Moreover, certain
measures were already being taken to facilitate remilitarisation: 'The presence in the Rhine plain of elements
of the *Landespolizei,* formations which are obviously
militarised, is such as to permit without delay the official
remilitarisation of the zone, since, on an order from
Berlin, these units could be immediately incorporated into
the army and equipped with appropriate artillery.'

Warned of the possibility the government neither postponed the ratification of the Franco-Soviet pact to deprive
Hitler of his pretext, nor took contingency action in
advance. When remilitarisation came their readiness to
take a stand, such as it was, was supported only by the
great conservative nationalist, Georges Mandel, and the
Socialist Paul-Boncour. In the country there was no
enthusiasm for action of any kind. On the Right the order
of the day, as given by *Action Française*, was 'Above all,
no war'. Amongst the Radicals there was no interest –
the local Radical Press passed over the affair in silence;
Paul Bastid, the Radical president of the Chamber's
Foreign Affairs Committee, refused to call a meeting
of his committee 'in order not to alarm the French people'.
The Socialists were intent on the avoidance of war.
Elections were in preparation and no one wanted to
intrude a divisive issue into a potentially tense domestic
situation. Subsequently, Paul-Boncour remembered
the situation in the cabinet when, in the most unimpres-
sive way, the last favourable moment for action was
allowed to pass: 'I saw M. Flandin, with his arm in a sling,
lean his great body towards the Prime Minister, whom
he was sitting beside, and say to him: "Prime Minister,
I see one ought not to insist."'

There was another aspect of the Rhineland crisis. The
British government's policy before the crisis had been
to seek an 'appeasement' of Europe to find a way of
satisfying both France and Germany, to meet those German demands which appeared not to constitute any threat
to Europe as a whole while at the same time providing
security for France. Hitler was well aware of this British
policy, and accompanied the Rhineland remilitarisation
with a variety of suggestions which accorded with British
notions of possible safeguards and guarantees – he talked
of a demilitarised zone on both sides of the frontier, a non-
aggression pact, an extension of the Locarno Pact, and the
air pact to which the British had attached so much importance. It was possible, therefore, for the London *Times* to
headline its editorial comment on the Rhineland remilitarisation 'A chance to rebuild'.

Flandin too knew what the British attitude was likely
to be. It is unlikely therefore that he expected to get from

the British government that degree of firmness which he could not secure — and scarcely tried to secure from his own Cabinet. His intention must have been rather to get the best possible support from Britain, on the assumption that the Rhineland would not be defended — to put the British government in the position of feeling duty-bound to offer France support because it had not backed the French over the Rhineland. The American chargé in London spotted the correct interpretation of Flandin's diplomacy when he reported: 'France must now put forward the most formidable demands in the hope of extracting something substantial out of the final compromise with England.'

In the end Flandin failed even in this limited objective. Nonetheless France had, by its abandonment of the Rhineland, handed the leadership in European policy to Britain. This was in part because it recognised the bankruptcy of its Eastern European policy. The days of the 1920s, when Briand had tried to get a British guarantee of the eastern frontiers of Germany and British support for the successor states, were past. Britain had refused to give any such commitments on the grounds that it did not have the military strength to do so; France had given the undertakings without backing them up with the necessary strategic or military planning. It was now apparent how hollow they were.

For all that, it was still possible for France to reassert her primacy. But her political weakness prevented her from doing so. In Britain the retirement of Baldwin in 1937 brought Neville Chamberlain to the premiership, with all the determined energy which, however misguided, characterised his career. In France it might be thought that the caretaker government of Albert Sarraut was as weak as could be found in a moment of national crisis. But when Hitler made his next aggressive move, in taking over Austria, France was without a government at all — possibly because Camille Chautemps, renowned for his skill in patching up compromises between parties and politicians, saw the crisis coming and resigned before it broke.

Left: *Cologne — smiling soldiers and welcoming civilians*

Chapter 5

The Popular Front

March 1936 was the month of Hitler's Rhineland coup. At the same time France was involved in an election campaign which for some represented a hope of a great political renewal and the opening of an era of reform, and for others represented the dire threat of Red Revolution. The parties of the Left had combined to present a common front to face Fascism and to win popular votes.

The Popular Front was born from the Stavisky riots; it was nurtured by the continuing menace of the Leagues, whose doctrines and organisation descended in part from a French tradition of authoritarianism and in part from foreign example. But these questions were unimportant to men who had witnessed the riots of 6th February and saw the mounting violence of demonstration through 1935. The Radical Party was above all a party which valued order. It had the paradoxical achievement of having reduced the upheaval of the Revolution to an orderly system of oratorical formulas, while its informal organisation concealed a strict sense of hierarchy and conventional behaviour. It is understandable that when, in the words of P.J.Larmour, 'thousands of Colonel de la Rocque's activists in their black leather jackets converged on a quiet provincial town, the Radical deputy felt that public order was being transgressed'.

The Socialists, more ideological than the Radicals and committed to peaceful behaviour (even though they formed into bands for self-protection against the Leagues), were equally offended and defensive. Their leader, Léon Blum, was vilified by the Right. 'The worst kind of Jew', he was called by Léon Daudet in *L'Action Française* — a man who, by being pacific, invited war and, by being a Jew, threatened to revive anti-Semitism. Nor were attacks of this sort purely verbal. Deputies were attacked: the Radical Paul Elbel had an eye knocked out at a political meeting in March 1935; Pierre Cot had acid thrown in his face two months later.

The Leagues themselves talked of taking power but

Left: Clenched fist salute and the hammer-and-sickle emblem — the French Left on the march to power via the Popular Front

never reached the point of doing so. At the end of 1935 one of their leaders, the right-wing deputy Ybarnégaray, went through a charade in the Chamber of Deputies, agreeing to dissolve the right-wing Leagues in return for the disbandment of the 'self-defence' groups of the Left. Laval, on the eve of his talks with Samuel Hoare, accepted the declaration of Ybarnégaray, Blum, and Thorez, the Communist, and introduced three bills banning paramilitary murder. The manoeuvre helped save Laval's government; but effective action against the Leagues only came when the Popular Front government was in power. Then, with commendable meekness, de la Rocque accepted the dissolution of the *Croix de Feu* as a League and turned it into an ordinary political party (of minor importance), the *Parti Social Français*.

But without the 'threat of Fascism', the constant talk by the Right of 'action', coup d'état, taking power, verbal threats, and vicious bullying, the alliance of the political parties would not have occurred. To the outsider such an alliance may appear natural, and it may be thought that the community of outlook between the progressive parties of the French Republic would make it an easy achievement. But thirty-five years after the Popular Front, the failure of the parties of the Left under the Fifth Republic to establish any degree of unity to compete with the Union of the Republic is evidence of the enduring nature of divisions of the Left.

Paradoxically, it was easier in some respects for the Radicals to join with the Communists than to join with the Socialists — in spite of earlier electoral alliances. They did not compete with the Communists for the same votes and to that extent less was at risk. As for the Communists, they stood to gain most from the Popular Front — and did. At the time of the split in the labour movement which followed the Russian Revolution they had a majority in the party congress. But they soon became a minority party — they took with them Jean Jaurès' newspaper *L'Humanité*, but had neither a mass following nor command over the trade union movement, only a splinter section, the *Confédération Générale du Travail Unitaire*. Some ground they had regained since then, but they inevitably appeared what they were — a party which took its orders from a foreign power.

The Popular Front provided a major opportunity, and made possible the growth in the Communist Party from then until the time when it established its command over

Right: The French Pandora releases the troubles of the 1936 elections. *Next page:* Communist poster attacks the financial Establishment. *Page 80:* Right-wing poster sees the traditional virtues — family, fatherland, work — threatened by socialism

La
CO

**POUR
L'APPLICATION
INTEGRALE DU PROGRAMM**
VOTEZ   CO

PARTI COMMUNISTE FRANÇAIS 120, rue Lafayette_PAR

Haute-Banque
tre la Nation
Ces hommes ne représentent ni le travail créateur, ni l'honnêteté de l'épargne, ni la technique de la production ; ils ne sont que les parasites de la bourse, de la spéculation et du profit.
MUNISTE
ÉLECTIONS CANTONALES 1937 Vu le candidat.

HAINE
DÉSORDRE
DUPERIE

PATRIE
FAMILLE
TRAVAIL

FRANÇAIS
CHOISISSEZ

Les Croix de Feu & Volontaires Nationaux

more than 20 per cent of the electorate after the Second World War. The Soviet Union joined the League of Nations in 1934 and, until the signature of the Nazi-Soviet pact in 1939, advocated the maintenance of collective security against Germany. In following the same line the French Communists were able to represent themselves as the best defence against Fascism. They laid the basis for the claim to represent French national interests — a claim which, in spite of their hostility to General de Gaulle in 1940, they were able to solidify in the Resistance once Germany attacked the Soviet Union.

The contrast between the Radical approach to the Popular Front and that of the Communists is thus striking. The Radical Party was the central party of the Third Republic, representative of many of its political qualities, providing its governments, having developed a genius for compromise — but grievously weakened by 6th February and its own abdication to Laval. It lacked clear ideology and the strength of its organisation rested on informal understanding and the peculiar links of the masonic order. The Communist Party could only gain power from an alliance. Its training gave it strength whenever questions of ideology were at issue, and over fifteen years it had constructed a disciplined organisation. Its political stance was changeable at a moment's notice on orders from Stalin; and in 1935-6 both ideology and organisation were suited to the needs of the moment. While the Radicals hesitated between Right and Left, self-reproachful over their right-wing alliance under Laval but dubious of their possible allies on the Left, the Communists had no rival on the Left and needed only to think of maximising their inroads into the traditional support of the Socialists and Radicals.

In the middle stood the Socialists. Since the split of 1920 they had grown steadily in numbers — membership stood at 35,000 in 1921 and reached 119,000 in 1929. Their newspaper, *Le Populaire,* never became a serious rival to the other great party newspapers, but they kept in addition a number of provincial dailies. The structure of the party meant that it repeatedly committed itself to programmes of a stylised nature — local and national congresses supported and voted for nationalisation, disarmament, peace, social reform, the forty-hour week. But what gave distinction to the party in the inter-war years was the outstanding personality of its leader, Léon Blum.

He was a man who could easily have made a successful career in law or in literature — indeed, he established his reputation before 1914 by his rapid promotion in the *Conseil d'Etat* and by his output as writer and critic. In 1919 he entered the Chamber of Deputies and gave up, professionally, both the law and literature. But his talent gave force to his politics. He established a fusion between the ideals of French democracy and the theories of Marxism, following a tradition already established by his friend Jean Jaurès. In a sense this rendered the party impotent – it could not choose the path of revolution, nor was it in a position to win a parliamentary majority. Its impotence was evident in its failure to join the left-wing governments of 1924 and 1932. But in compensation the members of the party had the reward of seeing their steadily growing numbers reflected in the size and importance of delegations to congresses as well as at the polls. Blum denounced the false ideals of a Communist revolution carried out before the necessary preparation in the political education of the people – revolution which could only lead therefore to dictatorship – and his argument was convincing in the period of growth of the party. The Communist leader, Maurice Thorez, may have laid claim to a more rigorously ideological (if changeable) doctrine but Blum more than made up for it by the force and clarity of his intellect. And above all he followed the dictum of the maverick writer with whom he had been associated at the time of the Dreyfus affair – Charles Péguy – that 'socialism will be moral, or it will not be at all'. In a political world not noted for its integrity the honesty of Blum was outstanding – and *L'Action Française* was driven the more to condemn his Jewishness through lack of moral charges to bring against him.

Party differences meant that the formation of the Popular Front was a slow and cumbersome affair. The first steps were taken on the Left, a week after the Stavisky riots, in a united Communist-Socialist demonstration on 12th February 1934. Four months' argument, dispute, and negotiation followed as Soviet foreign policy and Comintern directives changed their alignment. From trying to break up the Socialist Party by denunciation of the leadership which would win support from the ranks, the Communists turned towards a positive attempt to secure an alliance, attaching little importance to the ideological terms on which it might be formed. They met with a response from the Left of the Socialist Party, eager to form a union with the Communists, and a more cautious acceptance by the body of the party of the advantages to be gained in local elections from an alliance at the polls.

By the following year a combination of events hastened the momentum towards the Popular Front – increased Communist pressure now that the Franco-Soviet pact was signed; opposition to Laval; the approach of elections. Most important, the movement captured the

Right: Parisians study the various parties' propaganda, 1936

popular imagination. The climax came on Bastille Day, 1935. On that fourteenth of July the *Croix de Feu* marched down the Champs Elysées – an orderly and disciplined parade which carried little of the menace of 6th February. But from the populous areas of Paris a vast demonstration of people turned out to a mass meeting at Place de la Bastille. Revolutionaries linked arms with men of order – Daladier with Marty, who had organised mutinies in the French fleet at the end of the war, Blum and Thorez, Herriot with the Communist leaders Barbusse and Duclos. Their banners included those with the slogan Peace, Bread, Liberty – the winning words of the Bolshevik Revolution at the moment of Russia's defeat in 1917, singularly inappropriate to the practical realities of France in 1935.

With less than a year to go before the elections the trade union movement reunited into a single *Confédération Générale du Travail* – the prelude, as later events determined, of its takeover by the Communists. In January 1936 the programme of the Popular Front was published under three headings: Defence of Liberty, Defence of Peace, and Economic Demands. Old formulas – liberty of conscience in schools, the League of Nations, nationalisation of the armaments industry – were joined to a new and comprehensive programme for a forty-hour week, a national unemployment fund, and public works.

Victory for the Popular Front
With this programme the Popular Front went to the polls – two months after the Rhineland had been remilitarised. The Front was victorious. Between the government of the Right, still pursuing a deflationary policy and promising a 10% cut in civil service salaries, and the brave programme of the Popular Front the electorate had no difficulty in making its choice. It was possible to believe that a new start had been made in French political life, that a popular movement had carried itself into the Chamber and that, through the ballot box, the majority had demonstrated its will and aspirations – had symbolically invaded the Chamber as the Leagues, with their blustering and arrogance, had so signally failed to do. The appearance was deceptive.

The election itself represented a change in a distribution of the votes within the Left rather than a massive increase in the progressive vote. The elections of 1932 had themselves been a victory for the Left which the Stavisky riots and the practice of parliamentary politics had converted into a government of the Right. Four years later the combined parties of the Popular Front increased

Right: Offices of the Communist Party in the 1936 campaign

their percentage of the total popular vote by only 1.5%.

The changes between the parties were indeed momentous. The Radicals saw their share of the vote fall from 20 to 16.5% of the electorate. The Communists doubled their popular vote. The outcome in the Chamber was more striking still — it resulted from electoral alliances between the two ballots, in which the Communists participated for the first time. Electoral discipline was kept rigorously, except in a few constituencies where local rivalries were exceptionally strong (especially between Radicals and Socialists). The chief beneficiary of electoral alliances, the Communists, increased their representation in the Chamber from 10 to 72, while the Radicals lost 43 seats, tumbling from 159 to 116. The Socialist vote in total was extremely stable, although there were large increases in some constituencies balanced by decreases in others. (Some of the losses were to the Neo-Socialists — an authoritarian splinter group which had broken off in 1933 and looked increasingly similar to the authoritarians of the Right — but this was made up by gains on the Left.) What was important was that, with 146 seats, they emerged as the largest party in the Chamber.

The shift to the Left might be expected to produce both social reform and a more expansive economic policy. But in the event the Popular Front government was inflicted by blow after blow until the weight imposed on it was more than any government could carry — least of all one which was founded on the shifting sands of the Chamber of Deputies.

The first blow was struck in the formation of the government, when the Communists declined to participate in it. They had expected a Radical premier, and when, instead, Léon Blum invited them to join his Cabinet they lamely excused themselves. As a result their success at the polls brought the maximum instability to France. They could criticise the government and avoid taking responsibility for its shortcomings, or for the setbacks which it could not control. But at the same time the dramatic increase in the number of Communist deputies contributed largely to the sharp sense of alarm felt by the conservative and propertied classes.

Their fears were increased by the contagious spread through the country of strikes, which took the novel form of sitting in the factories. The outbreak, beginning in the Paris metallurgical industry on 24th May and spreading across the country, was spontaneous, prompted by the simple impatience of workers for the reform which the Popular Front had promised, accompanied by a sense of euphoria as a result of the victory won. Unorganised at

Right: Maurice Thorez (centre), leader of the Communist Party

the start, they were to some extent taken over by the Communists, anxious not to lose an opportunity to assert their leadership.

The strikes served a useful purpose. The employers were sufficiently alarmed for Blum to be able to extract agreements, signed in the new premier's residence, the Hôtel Matignon (in the Rue de Varenne) and named accordingly. The agreements were a landmark in the development of working-class legislation: they guaranteed a forty-hour week, paid holidays, and collective bargaining. With the help of Maurice Thorez, the strikers were persuaded to return to work.

To the extent that the rights of the working class had been advanced and guaranteed in legislation a victory could be thought to have been won. But the price paid for the forty-hour week was no less than a major contribution to the collapse of the Popular Front and an additional source of military weakness when war broke out. Tragically, neither Blum nor his advisers had a better understanding of economics than their right-wing opponents, and both sides saw the issues in terms of emotional politics to the total neglect of technical economics. This in part explains the curiously sporadic nature of social and economic legislation. The Bank of France was reformed, thus implementing the slogan *'Faire de la Banque de France "la Banque de la France"'*. Its General Assembly, drawn from the two hundred largest shareholders, was enlarged to include all shareholders, and the governing council reformed. Another slogan was thus put into legislation—the '200 families' had, it was believed, controlled the destinies of France. A mixture of pacificism and socialism brought the nationalisation of the armaments industry—it was left to the Chautemps government, in August 1937, to nationalise the railways and set up the SNCF. A Wheat Office was established in order to control the price and sale of wheat, as well as to act as sole agent for its import.

To the extent that a single theme inspired economic reforms it was the disastrous, and false, assumption that there was a fund of work to be distributed. For the justification of the forty-hour week was not that workers were over-worked—the average working week varied from forty-four to forty-eight hours—but that in this way unemployment would be reduced. In the same way the school-leaving age was raised, both to equip school-leavers with greater skill and, again, to reduce unemployment.

Neither simple nor complex remedies were sought to expand production. The most desirable simple remedy

Right: *Socialist premier Léon Blum, head of the Popular Front*

was still that which Paul Reynaud had proposed – devaluation. But for Blum, as for the majority of his contemporaries, devaluation meant a deprivation – almost the theft of part of the value of money. It was not understood as part of economic dynamics. He, therefore, took his stand – as the leaders of other left-wing governments were to do after him – and stated in evocative terms: 'The country should not expect from us, nor fear from us, our covering the walls some fine morning with the white notices announcing devaluation.'

As a result, the disequilibrium between the French economy and that of the world, which had played so small a part in the reasoning of the leaders of the Popular Front, increased. There was an adverse balance of payments, French prices rose faster than world prices, and there was a constant outflow of gold both to cover the balance of payments and as the result of panic inspired by the very existence of the Popular Front, backed up by the intemperate strikers. In September 1936 Blum found it impossible to resist devaluation any longer. The Stock Exchange was closed, convertibility suspended and an embargo placed on the export of gold. On 28th September the franc was devalued by approximately 25 per cent. The law necessary to effect the devaluation passed easily in the Chamber, but in the Senate – ominously – by a majority of only ten votes.

Devaluation brought an immediate revival of the economy. But as it did so the forty-hour week began to be introduced in major industries. The result was an artificial barrier to increased production, at a time when the opportunity opened itself for economic expansion. Industrial production rapidly levelled off, taxation failed to produce increased revenue, and – again in large part for psychological rather than economic reasons – gold flowed out of the country once more.

Less than a year after coming to power Léon Blum's government found itself forced to slow down its programme of reform and ask for a 'pause' in the implementation of its promises – it postponed the introduction of old-age pensions and the adjustment of wages to the cost of living and reduced the programme of public works. Doing so, it was inevitably attacked by the Communists, and their strictures found echoes on the Left of the Socialist party. These recriminations were added to those brought against the government for its failure to assist the Republican government of Spain against the insurgence of General Franco.

Left: June 1937: the army distributes bread during a bakers' strike – the establishment of a Popular Front government did not spell an end to industrial unrest and class warfare

At first sight it must seem that every consideration would compel the Popular Front government to lend support to the Spanish government – a government too of *Frente Popular*. Defence against Fascism had been a powerful emotive force in France; across the Pyrenees the government was engaged in military defence against a military, authoritarian, and Fascist uprising. On less ideological grounds the Spanish government had the right of any government to purchase arms for its own defence, and a trade treaty of 1935 with France made provision for such purchase.

When, on 20th July 1936, Blum received a telegram from the Spanish Prime Minister, José Giral, seeking aid against the insurrection, which had started two days previously, his immediate reaction was indeed to accede to it. But his instincts were not those either of the British government or of many of his own ministers. The British were strongly opposed to any form of intervention in Spain and ready to restrain the French if necessary. Blum's cabinet was divided, with both Radicals and Socialists warning of the division which would be created in the country if support were given to the Spanish government.

In their prognosis they were undoubtedly correct: the fear of the Right that France would be drawn into war on the wrong side was enhanced by the Spanish Civil War. Inevitably their sympathies were with Franco, defender of their values – and their Church – against the tyranny of the Left. Pressure from Britain was also important to Blum – distrustful of Russia and rejecting Laval's Italian policy he attached great value to the alignment of British and French foreign policy.

In spite of this Blum himself attached sufficient importance to Spain to consider resignation. It was the Spanish government itself which released him from this obligation, by urging that the break-up of the Popular Front in France would be a graver blow than the failure to supply arms. No doubt their calculations changed as Italian aid to Franco increased; but correspondingly so did the pressure on Blum to avoid the danger of international war over Spain. As the days passed at the end of July and beginning of August 1936 Blum was increasingly isolated in his own Cabinet and finally acquiesced in the only alternative to resignation – the support of a policy of non-intervention. Thereafter only very limited supplies of French arms reached Spain – either via Mexico, or clandestinely, with the connivance of the customs, across the Pyrenees.

Right: *Just arrived from Spain, French veterans of the struggle against Franco's fascists parade through the streets of Paris*

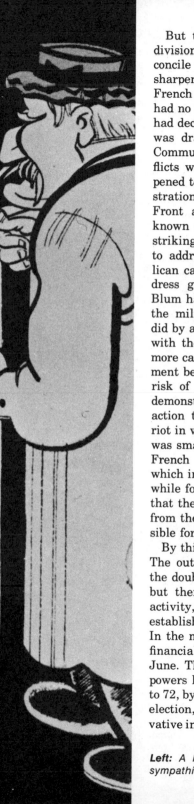

But the policy of non-intervention did not eliminate division within France. It was insufficient by itself to reconcile the Right to a Popular Front government, and it sharpened the divisions within the Left, and within the French Socialist Party. On these points the Communists had no inhibitions in attacking a government which they had declined to join, while the Left of the Socialist Party was drawn away from the government, preferring its Communist allies to the Radicals. Inevitably, these conflicts were projected into the streets. Nothing had happened to break the habit of popular agitation and demonstration built up during the making of the Popular Front and then the sit-in strikes. Dolores Ibarruri – known as *la Pasionaria* ('Passion Flower') and the most striking of the Spanish Communists – came from Spain to address meetings in support of the Spanish Republican cause, her grave, fanatical face and austere black dress giving her the aspect of a revolutionary saint. Blum had to justify his policy of non-intervention before the militants and masses of his own party – which he did by an emotional appeal, identifying non-intervention with the preservation of peace. But with the return to more cautious economic policies in the spring the government became doubly vulnerable to left-wing attack. The risk of violence which is always attendant on popular demonstration became more real, and in March 1937 police action to control a crowd in the Place Clichy led to a riot in which seven people were killed. In scale the clash was small; but on the Left it awoke memories of earlier French governments claiming to be revolutionary, which in 1848 and 1871 had turned guns on the workers; while for many Radicals with short memories it showed that the danger was no longer from Fascist Leagues but from the Communists, whom they believed to be responsible for the deaths that had occurred.

By this time the government was reaching an impasse. The outflow of gold continued – at first merely showing the doubts of the wealthy for the future of their country but then, with the continuing weakness of industrial activity, becoming large enough to threaten the fund established to hold the new exchange level of the franc. In the middle of June Blum asked the Chamber for full financial powers to deal with the crisis, until the end of June. The Chamber of Deputies supported him; but the powers he asked for were rejected outright, by 188 votes to 72, by the Senate which, elected by a system of indirect election, represented all that was cautious and conservative in French political life. Blum resigned.

Left: A French cartoon illustrates the confusion of political sympathies and allegiances in the Popular Front government

But he would not admit failure. The pretence that the Popular Front still existed – and that economic recovery was under way – was kept up. In fact its failure went deep. The alliance of the Popular Front was, as we have seen, slow in the making. When it broke, it was inevitable that scapegoats would be found and recriminations let loose. This was particularly true of the attitude of many Radicals towards the Communists, and it was given full rein when the Communist Party was suppressed by Daladier's government after the conclusion of the Nazi-Soviet pact. The government had excited alarm amounting to panic on the Right, who were incapable of recognising that Blum, weak as he may have been in economic skills, believed passionately that his government was responsible for the future of France, not for a class or a party. Had Blum been working in a different political system it is possible, although by no means certain, that he would have been able to maintain his authority intact over a period of four or five years, to survive setback and regain popularity through an upswing of the economy. But the arrangements and the conventions of the Third Republic were such that the break-up of his government left a greater loss of confidence, a diminished sense of loyalty to the Republic, a loss of direction which prepared the way for the Vichy government three years later.

Nor had the Popular Front emasculated the anti-parliamentarian forces in French politics. On the contrary, its coming to power saw the birth at the same time of Jacques Doriot's *Parti Populaire Français* – a party closer to Fascism and more important than the *Francist* party, and a sinister secret society which hatched a detailed plan for a coup d'état.

Jacques Doriot started his political career as a Communist – joining the Party in the first year of its existence in 1920 when he was twenty-two. Violent and audacious in his political campaigning, he was able to maintain a virtuosity which did not fit easily into the increasing discipline of the 1920s but which his seductive leadership – in the Party and as a young deputy – made irrepressible. But at the time of the Stavisky scandal the gap between Doriot and the Party widened: Doriot pressed for unity of action with the Socialists. Within a very short time the Party changed its policy

*Right: Cooperative movement appeals to the French worker. **Next page, left:** France awaits the verdict on her Popular Front government from an 'international court' (MacDonald, Hitler, Mussolini, and Roosevelt). **Next page, right:** French nationalist poster shows a Gaul warding off attacks from Communism, Nazism, Socialism, and Freemasonry. **Page 100:** 'Help Spain', cover of a French pro-Loyalist pamphlet by Miro*

TU ES SYNDIQUÉ ? POURQUO N'ES TU PAS COOPÉRATEUR

COOPERATIVE

MAGASIN UNIVERSEL

SALLE DE LE

RESTAURANT COOPÉRATIF

ŒUVRES SO

L'ACCUSÉE

and adopted that of Doriot. But before it did so Doriot was expelled by the International, in spite of having overwhelming support from his own constituency. Within two years he had become as violent in his hostility to Communism as previously he had opposed colonialism. In June 1936 the *Parti Populaire Français* was established in the Paris suburb of St Denis.

The party had the outward signs of a Fascist party — its flag, its salute, and its hymn. Its doctrine was nationalist and socialist. It appropriated the nationalist symbols of both Right and Left — both Joan of Arc and the great Feast of the Federations in 1790 — and it denounced (as Hitler had done before he saw the support to be gained from sympathetic industrialists) the 'capitalism of trusts, great centralised businesses, the capitalism of joint stock companies, boards of directors, banks'. It became increasingly anti-Semitic. The party had an important mass following — its newspaper, *L'Emancipation nationale,* printed 200,000 copies; it claimed 137,000 members and certainly could fill the *Vélodrome d'Hiver,* the biggest Paris hall, with a capacity of between fifty and sixty thousand. And Doriot, in true Fascist pattern, was a leader whose will was expected to prevail because he claimed that it emanated from the masses.

A different organisation came into existence at the same time as the PPF — the *Comité Secret d'Action Révolutionnaire.* Its membership was drawn in part from *Action Française,* in part from those members of the *Croix de Feu* who were not prepared to accept either the procrastination of de la Rocque or the metamorphosis of the League into a political party. Its leader, Eugène Deloncle, was a consultant naval engineer and company director who had been a member of the *Action Française.* It made no secret of its aim to anticipate the Communist revolution (which it believed to be imminent) by a coup of its own, and actively prepared for the event. It acquired a vast quantity of armaments from Italy and Spain.

The organisation had all the attractions of a secret society and its members probably enjoyed the contemptuous soubriquet given them by Maurice Pujo of the *Action Française* — he called them the *cagoulards* (hooded men). But it was as sinister as such a society can be. Indiscipline was punishable by death — and such sentences were carried out. Obligingly, being admirers of Mussolini, *cagoulards* murdered two refugees at the behest of the Italian security service.

The PPF never fought an election nor did the *cagoulards* carry out their coup. The Socialist minister, Marx Dormoy, dismissed Doriot from the mayoralty of St Denis and uncovered the *cagoulard* conspiracy in November 1937. But they provided an infrastructure for the collaboration of Vichy with Nazi Germany.

Chapter 6
The Approach to War

Whatever estimate one makes of the success and failure of the Popular Front government the contrast with events in Germany remains terrifying. The Popular Front was preoccupied with the threat of Fascism in France and then became divided further by events across the border in Spain. But the real threat, quite disproportionately greater than the menace of Fascism internally, came from across the Rhine. The success of the Nazi regime meant that a nation nearly twice as populous as the French, well endowed with natural resources and even better equipped with an industrial base, was being organised to achieve the maximum output and, above all, to rearm. German production was probably 30 per cent higher in 1938 than in 1930; in France production fell with the introduction of the forty-hour week – steel production was 68 per cent of the 1928 level in 1936, rose to 82 per cent in 1937, and fell back to 64 per cent in 1938.

The Popular Front government was aware of the danger which Germany represented: it produced in Blum the same kind of crisis of conscience as did the civil war in Spain. He had an abhorrence of war and was committed to a policy of disarmament and peace. As he said in justifying non-intervention in Spain, 'You understand me very well: everything to avert the present and future risk of war. I refuse to consider war as possible today because it might be necessary or inevitable tomorrow. War is possible only when one admits it to be possible; inevitable when one proclaims it to be inevitable. As for myself, until the last, I refuse to despair of peace and of the action of the French nation for the preservation of peace.'

In the life of Blum's government there was no international crisis, except for the Spanish Civil War, which called for the exercise of diplomacy. But in the pursuit of peace he welcomed the visit in August 1936 of Hjalmar Schacht, Hitler's Minister of Finance and Economics, in the hope that it would open up the possibility of

Left: 'Tomorrow, this will be our fate if . . .' – poster warns of possible consequences of Popular Front pacifist leanings

discussions with Germany, and he made clear in public speeches that he would enter into negotiations of any sort which might produce a reconciliation of French and German views. Not until 1938 did his optimism and his fundamental belief in the natural goodness and rationality of man yield before the accumulating evidence of the aggressive nature of Hitler's regime.

Long before that, however, he had pressed forward with increased rearmament. Military service had been extended to two years in March 1935; the arms budget was doubled from 1936 to 1937, rising to nearly three billion francs—in 1938 it was more than five billion. Obviously, however, the mere expenditure of money did not suffice to equip France's defences to be a match for Germany. The task was exacting enough under the best of circumstances—the need for self-defence was thrust upon France, whereas the expansion of Germany and the construction of armed forces to achieve this objective remained Hitler's central purpose. He could choose his time—and did so with genius—and his mode of attack.

But almost everything in France militated against a successful armaments policy, except for the existence of technical skill, which by itself was useless. During the coming war the Vichy government sought to lay the blame for the failure of rearmament at the door of the Popular Front; but having charged Blum and his colleagues and embarked on a trial at Riom the prosecutors had to abandon their attack in the face of the evidence of the failures of the military. The politicians, it is true, did not take up the ideas which had been put forward in Britain by Liddell Hart and taken up in Germany by General Guderian. In 1934 Captain de Gaulle published *Vers l'Armée de Métier* in which he revealed his own conversion to the importance of a quickly moving manoeuvrable army. But his argument was not only one of strategy: he insisted equally strongly on the need to create a professional corps of élite troops. His proposals were bound to raise political objections which obscured their purely military aspects; for an essential part of the republican tradition was belief in an 'army of the people' rather than a professional force which might carry out a coup d'état. In spite of this it was primarily because of strategic myopia that the politicians—with the exception of Reynaud, who had preceded de Gaulle by ten years in pressing for a mobile army—ruled de Gaulle's ideas out of court. But whatever their responsibility, that of the generals, whose job it was to advise the

Left: *British minister Hore-Belisha (civilian on the left) with Daladier as spectators at the French army manoeuvres of 1937*

civilians, is greater. With all the intelligence evidence of Guderian's panzer divisions available to them, with the demonstration of German tactics in the Spanish Civil War, they were unwilling to learn the lessons of mechanised warfare. 'Oil is dirty, dung is not' was their belief, one which even the Polish campaign of 1939 could not shake.

From a purely technical standpoint French armament had much that was unsurpassed. The Maginot Line was, by itself, the outstanding example. Begun in 1930, it was intended that it should be completed by 1935, when the last occupation zone of Germany was to be evacuated (in fact evacuation was completed in 1930). It was to run from near the Swiss border to Longwy, close to the meeting point of the Belgian and Luxembourg frontiers. The forts which constituted its strongpoints were in the best tradition of military engineering in which the French had excelled since the time of Vauban. Alistair Horne, in *To Lose a Battle,* describes them thus: 'When troops passed through their cavernous gates, placed discreetly at the base of some hill, they entered into a Wellsian civilisation in which they could live, sleep, eat, work, and exercise for many weeks without ever seeing the surface of the earth – not unlike nuclear submariners of today embarking on a voyage under the Pole. Electric trains whisked them from their underground barracks and canteens to their gun turrets; vast power stations, equally underground, provided them with heat and light; powerful compressor plants supplied them with air, and ensured that the forts were proof against poison gas; immense subterranean food stores, reservoirs, and fuel tanks would enable them to remain cut off from the rest of the French army for up to three months.'

The Maginot Line was the outstanding but not the only example of technical excellence. The Dewoitine fighter of the mid-thirties was superb – but out of date both in the craftsman-type production it called for and in its performance by the time war broke out. The Somua and the B-type tanks, however, surpassed those which Hitler was producing at the same time.

Technical quality, however, is useless by itself – even dangerously useless. The Maginot Line absorbed a disproportionate amount of the credits available for armaments during the years of deflation. Its purely defensive structure and its failure to cover the Belgian frontier have often been commented on. The contrast with the line which the Germans started constructing after the remilitarisation of the Rhineland emphasises the point.

Left: *The Maginot Line – a relief column marches along one of its underground chambers (note the several railway tracks)*

The two lines faced each other, both leaving a gap to the north, on the French side from Longwy to the sea. The German command was to use this gap for its main attack, while their Siegfried Line strengthened the defence, weaker in manpower, in the centre. The French command had no plans for offensive action associated with their defensive line and were unable to cover the northern sector. Initially, they had assumed that the Belgian defences would provide forward cover. The Belgian pursuit of neutrality after the remilitarisation of the Rhineland made it impossible for the French to concert plans with the Belgian army, even when war broke out in 1939; but they lacked both the resolve and the money to pursue the alternative course of extending the Maginot Line to cover the Belgian frontier.

If strategic planning was weak, so too was the support for the armed forces from the country's industrial base. The fault here lies with the political system rather than with individual ministers. It has frequently — and mis-leadingly — been said that the competence of the French civil service compensated, under the Third and Fourth Republics, for the instability of governments. That the civil service ensured the continuity of efficient adminis-tration there can be no doubt; but decisions as to which aircraft to produce in order to have a balanced air force with the most advanced machines at the right moment call for a combination of expert advice and political decision. Instead the French air force was subjected to changing governments and a Popular Front minister (Pierre Cot) who was more interested in international disarmament and nationalisation than the production of aeroplanes. The aircraft industry had scarcely begun to adapt itself to mass production before it was sub-jected to the reforms of the Popular Front, including the forty-hour week.

French military weakness was of decisive importance when the battle was joined in 1940. It played a deter-minant part before then to the extent that it contributed to the growth of defeatism — a phenomenon which scarcely existed in Britain, for all that the British government and people led the French in the attempt to avoid war. It made French military leaders and civilian politicians — General Vuillemin, commander-in-chief of the air force, and Georges Bonnet chief amongst them — vulnerable to the mixture of bravado and actual military strength which the Nazis deployed to alarm their enemies. The French came to believe, not only that they were not strong enough to defend their allies, but that they were too weak to avoid conquest themselves.

Left: *Transporting food to troops stationed in the Maginot Line*

Moreover political life in France continued to be dominated by social conflict and political instability. The German dynamo was turning with ever-increasing force; even Britain began to experience economic recovery and, more important, had a stable government headed by an activist, energetic Prime Minister. In France the fall of the Popular Front government was followed by the continuing decline of the Front itself. Blum's government was succeeded by one headed by Chautemps. The Socialists continued to participate, but the Radicals had now taken the lead. At the end of 1937 there was a massive strike in the Goodrich tyre factory, another in the public services of the Paris district (including buses and the metro), which had been unaffected by the great strikes of 1936. A public strike of this sort was a major embarrassment for the Socialist Minister of the Interior. In acting against the *Cagoule* he was politically on more natural ground. But the placing of bombs in the offices of the Employers' Association *(Confédération Générale du Patronat français)* and the headquarters of the Union of Mechanical Industries, for which the *Cagoule* were held responsible, and the uncovering of their plans for a coup d'état added to the sense of conspiracy and conflict.

Meanwhile the alliance of the Popular Front was becoming increasingly difficult to maintain. Once its first unity was broken the Radicals followed their normal practice in reconsidering their alliances, without wanting to be the first to make a formal break. The signs were obvious when Daladier protested (probably without justification) about the way the Socialists had played their electoral alliances in the cantonal elections of the autumn of 1937; 'if class discipline is put ahead of republican discipline', he said, 'then we will have to take our freedom of action without hesitation'. In the following months the financial situation again deteriorated with the outflow of capital and Chautemps manoeuvred his government towards resignation in January 1938.

In the constitutional crisis that followed Léon Blum was amongst those who were asked to form a government. He showed his own sense of national emergency by trying to construct a cabinet broader than that of the Popular Front—it was to go from the Left to the Right of the political spectrum—'from Thorez to Reynaud'. His attempt failed, and rebounded. Once Blum showed dissatisfaction with the orthodox Popular Front the Radicals felt liberated from any obligation and Chautemps formed a new government, this time without Socialist participation. It lasted from the end of January until March

Right: Outbreaks of violence continue—headquarters of the Employers' Association in Paris, wrecked by a bomb in 1937

1938, when it resigned over problems of financial legislation. Blum formed a further government which was even shorter: once again he sought a national alliance, and when it failed, tried to reconstruct the Popular Front. But this government, like Blum's first Ministry, failed to secure a majority and resigned.

Between the second Chautemps government and that of Blum occurred the *Anschluss,* forced on Austria by Hitler, accompanied by the invasion of Austria by German panzer divisions (although the SS preceded them and began rounding up the Jews of Vienna). There was no government in office to react to the event, and the attention of those who had left one government or were to join the next was taken up with the customary *va-et-vient* of cabinet-making. Strikingly, Georges Bonnet, who had been Minister of Finance, was to become Foreign Minister and was amongst the possible Premiers in 1938 —describes the sequence in his Memoirs as *'Trois crises en trois mois'* — all the crises, naturally, being those of the government, none of the nation.

But for all that the *Anschluss* had a profound impact on French politics. In the two years that had passed since the Rhineland crisis, domestic affairs had been paramount. The attempts of the government to escape from the restrictions of the forty-hour week brought massive resistance from organised workers who saw their first major gains in collective bargaining under attack — and still thought longer hours meant fewer employed. Workers in the aircraft industry went on strike (thus stopping the delivery of aeroplanes); so did those in the Renault factories. Each of these genuine problems of government became in addition a problem of political alliances between the parties.

After the *Anschluss* attention was inevitably turned to Germany, and it was now that the defection of the Right from their traditional nationalist attitude to Germany was of decisive importance. The Popular Front, by common consent, was broken and everyone looked for a government of National Union. But such a government, if it was to offer resistance to Germany, could only be based on a coalition of the kind which had inspired the *Réveil national* before 1914. Instead the Right had become at best defensive and at worst ready to prefer Hitler to the Communists. 'Let us not go into heroics about Austria, let us take refuge behind our Maginot Line,' said Flandin, while *L'Action Française* propagated the theme: 'Nothing for a war of doctrine. All for the defence of our sacred soil.'

Right: Bastille Day (14th July), 1938 — a Communist banner proclaims that in defending the Soviet Union the French working-class is also helping to defend its own interests

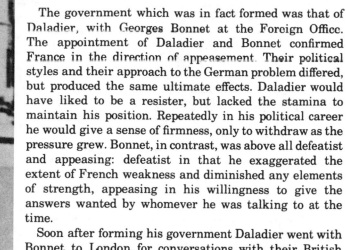

The government which was in fact formed was that of Daladier, with Georges Bonnet at the Foreign Office. The appointment of Daladier and Bonnet confirmed France in the direction of appeasement. Their political styles and their approach to the German problem differed, but produced the same ultimate effects. Daladier would have liked to be a resister, but lacked the stamina to maintain his position. Repeatedly in his political career he would give a sense of firmness, only to withdraw as the pressure grew. Bonnet, in contrast, was above all defeatist and appeasing: defeatist in that he exaggerated the extent of French weakness and diminished any elements of strength, appeasing in his willingness to give the answers wanted by whomever he was talking to at the time.

Soon after forming his government Daladier went with Bonnet to London for conversations with their British counterparts. The record of their conversation gives the impression of French foresight meeting British complacency and reluctance to take any stand against Germany. The French ministers urged the danger to Czechoslovakia and pressed the British to join with them in formulating a common policy. 'If we allowed Germany a new success every month or three months till she achieved a hegemony, she would turn on the West', said Daladier. 'If there were no signs of a determined policy and a common agreement between the British and French governments, they would have sealed the fate of Europe.'

They received little encouragement from the British. Chamberlain questioned whether Hitler intended the break-up of Czechoslovakia and was not therefore prepared to go to its defence. Since coming to power his government had sought the means to reach a 'general settlement with Germany'. Increasingly the Czechs would appear as standing in the way of such a settlement.

Would French action have been different had they received support from Britain? Could the British government have reversed the trend towards defeatism and appeasement? The possibility cannot be ruled out. The French cabinet was divided. The advocates of resistance included Paul Reynaud, Georges Mandel, Champetier de Ribes, Campinchi, Zay, and Queuille, Daladier at first hovered between them and the defeatists—de Monzie, Pomaret, and Chautemps in addition to Bonnet. On balance it is unlikely. No doubt when Daladier and Bonnet came to London they hoped that with sufficiently strong words from Britain and France together Hitler's pressure on Czechoslovakia would weaken and the crisis

Left: Hitler enters Austria 1938—France was given no rest from the ambitions of her dynamic and acquisitive Nazi neighbour

disappear. In fact, this would not have happened without at least a degree of determined and prolonged resistance of which the French ministers, in their insecure political environment, were not capable.

Between Hitler's determination and the optimistic British hopes of reaching a settlement it was inevitable that France would be brought up against the responsibilities of the defensive alliance signed with Czechoslovakia in 1925. Daladier and Bonnet did not have the freedom of manoeuvre which the British believed was theirs. They were committed to go to the defence of Czechoslovakia in the event of attack. More than that, the alliance was part of the Eastern European policy of the 1920s, framed on the presupposition that France was a major European power with responsibility for the maintenance of the treaty settlement in Europe. The abandonment of Czechoslovakia meant the abandonment of French greatness.

The British government were well aware of the French dilemma, although they had little sympathy for it. The Foreign Secretary, Lord Halifax, explained to the Cabinet that 'The French obligation to Czechoslovakia dated from a time when Germany was disarmed. In present circumstances it was desirable, if possible, to obtain a release for the French from their obligations.' This objective would be achieved if a compromise could be reached which the Czechs themselves would accept.

'Two bites at the cherry'

The pattern of diplomacy was thus established. The French ministers had come to London apparently in search of a joint policy towards Germany which would enable Britain and France to regain the initiative. In the event the initiative rested with Hitler who could, had he so desired, have dismantled the Czech crisis, or invaded the country, or—as was in fact the case—settled for two bites at the cherry. It was the British who led in the diplomacy designed to counter Hitler's moves by a series of initiatives culminating in Chamberlain's decision to implement his 'plan Z', i.e. to fly to meet Hitler in Germany. There was no joint diplomacy towards Berlin—only towards Prague, where the British enlisted French support to bring pressure on the Czech government to accept the demands which they formulated in the hope of buying off Hitler.

As the temperature of the international crisis increased, so Daladier became more irresolute and Bonnet more determined to avoid war. When Hitler addressed the party-day rally at Nuremberg on 12th September his intentions towards Czechoslovakia became abundantly clear. The British Ambassador in Paris reported home that he found Bonnet 'in a state of collapse' and 'thoroughly cowed'. Daladier for his part tried frantically to get in touch with London: he could not bring himself to bow to Hitler and wanted Chamberlain to do it for him, so that some way out could be found between the choice for France of failing in her obligations to Czechoslovakia and going to war. At this point the capitulation of the French helped precipitate Chamberlain's decision to fly to meet Hitler at Berchtesgaden, on 15th September.

It was impossible however for the French to abrogate responsibility completely to Britain. When they flew to London after Chamberlain's first meeting with Hitler the plan they drew up was an Anglo-French plan, and the British insisted on their support in presenting it to Prague. In return the French ministers insisted that Czechoslovakia — dismembered by the cession of the Sudeten lands to Germany — should be given a new guarantee, by Britain as well as by France. This scarcely accorded with British plans — it was not their intention, having escaped from the Franco-Czech alliance, to enter a commitment in Central Europe themselves. In the end they agreed that Czechoslovakia should be given such a guarantee, on condition that she accepted 'a position of neutrality' and agreed 'to act on our advice on issues of peace and war'.

A week after Berchtesgaden Chamberlain flew a second time to see Hitler. He went in a mood of optimism. He had kept control of the diplomacy between the British, French, and Czechs; the British and French had agreed in principle to the secession of the Sudetenland to Germany and had secured Czech acceptance of the Anglo-French plan. Indeed, he had been more successful than Hitler had imagined possible.

Hitler appears to have assumed that the British and French would find a way out for themselves, but that the Czechs would refuse to yield the Sudetenland, so that he would have the pretext to 'crush' Czechoslovakia without running the risk of general war. It was this which produced his thoroughly aggressive posture and his demands for immediate military occupation. In fact, the opposite proved the case: he could have the Sudetenland without fighting anyone, but he could crush Czechoslovakia only at the risk of war, for as Chamberlain returned to England both Britain and France intensified the preparations they had made — mobilising the fleet and manning the Maginot Line. At the same time Chamberlain despatched his representative, Sir Horace Wilson,

Left: Architects of appeasement — Lord Halifax, British Foreign Secretary (right), and Sir John Simon, ex-Foreign Secretary

to convey to Hitler that 'if, in pursuit of her treaty obligations, France became actively engaged in hostilities against Germany, the United Kingdom would feel obliged to support her'

Undoubtedly this was a major factor in persuading Hitler to accept what he was offered and, for the time being, to avoid war. At his most vitriolic Hitler had left a door open to Chamberlain – this strange man who was ready to concede so much but was impervious to personal bullying – and Chamberlain would neglect no last chance for peace. So, with the assistance of Mussolini, a further conference at Munich was arranged between Chamberlain, Daladier, Hitler, and Mussolini. It produced the famous Munich agreement, which provided, as far as the first zone of the Sudetenland was concerned, for the immediate occupation (on 1st October) which Hitler had demanded, with complete occupation to follow within ten days.

The sequence of diplomacy brought out sharply the contrast between Daladier and Bonnet. The former would almost have welcomed being forced into a position of resistance; instead he found himself accepting the Munich agreement and, weary and defeated, sank into the depths of despair. Bonnet in contrast was indefatigable in the cause of peace, in the sense that he resisted any suggestion that Britain and France might have to fight. He did everything in his power to convey to Hitler that if he were denied some of his objectives now he would be able to secure them, without fighting, later.

What politicians shared with ordinary people was the sense of relief which followed from having gone to bed on 27th September in the belief that the outbreak of war, with all the nightmares they had conjured up of aerial bombardment, was immediately imminent, to discover the next day that there was after all a hope of peace and to learn on the day after that of the signature of an agreement. Daladier did not foresee the welcome that would await him on his return – a spontaneous outpouring of emotion which Georges Bonnet's planning had helped to channel to maximum effect. That he should have been so astonished was in part the result of the absence of parliamentary discussion during the course of the crisis. Neville Chamberlain had repeatedly reported his activities to the House of Commons, and was able to enjoy the full effect of receiving Hitler's agreement to a four-power conference actually in the House while he was in the middle of a speech. In France the Chamber of Deputies was in recess and the repeated requests that par-

Left: Edouard Daladier signs the Munich Agreement for France

liament should be recalled were rejected by the government. On 4th October the Chamber at last met, to hear a statement by Daladier which lacked the detail of Chamberlain's statements and was unsupported by any documents. After a debate of six hours, in which the Communists and Henri de Kerillis, a lone figure on the Right and editor of the independent newspaper *L'Epoque,* attacked the agreement, the government was given a vote of confidence by 543 votes to 75.

The Communists alone as a major party voted against the agreement; their later success in posing as a patriotic party owed much to the integrity of their position. In the short run they became the whipping boys for the Radicals who, now that the Popular Front was finally broken, vented their pent-up emotions on the Communist Party. The Socialists were divided. Léon Blum was too honest not to be aware of the sacrifice which had been made, and too much a lover of peace not to say, on 1st October: 'There is not a man or woman in France who can refuse to Mr Chamberlain and Edouard Daladier his just tribute of gratitude.' Against Blum the secretary-general of the party, Paul Faure, was unequivocal in support of appeasement, and became a life-long friend of Bonnet as a result of the crisis. Marx Dormoy, in contrast, wrote, 'Peace at any price is inevitably war at any price . . . we will find peace by justice and by force. Alas! Yes, force. For those who oppose us will yield only to that.' The division was a prelude to that which would occur in the moment of defeat; for the resisters a sense of shame not only spurred them during the occupation but lived on to inspire their policy towards Algeria and Egypt.

As for the Right, its abdication was virtually complete. Henri de Kerillis, almost alone in the right-wing Press, carried the banner of traditional nationalism. Flandin sent a telegram to Hitler, and was embarrassed that the reply, sent through the ordinary telegraph service, was no secret to the postal employees who handled it or to anyone else. When white posters appeared on 23rd September calling reservists to arms they were pasted over with handbills reading: *'Français on vous trompe. Pas de chantage au patriotisme'* ('Frenchmen, you are being deceived. No patriotic blackmail'). *Action Française,* condemned, it should be remembered, by the Church and rejected by the royal pretender, provided new words to the tune of the *Internationale:*

> If they insist these cannibals
> On making us heroes
> Our first bullets must be
> For Mandel, Blum and Reynaud.

Left: *In the aftermath of Munich, relieved Frenchmen toast peace*

— Sont-ils trop verts ?...

Isolated individuals like Jacques Duhamel and Louis Marin expressed their awareness of what had been given away. The resisters in the cabinet expressed their intention to resign more than once, but were persuaded to stay. Churchill urged his friend Mandel that resignation would make no difference to the course of events and would only destroy morale. Over the nation as a whole settled an immense feeling of relief — and also, no doubt, humiliation.

In the remaining months of 1938 Daladier and Bonnet showed their different aspects in events of relatively minor importance. After Munich the French Ambassador to Berlin, François-Poncet, whose reports are marked by their clear assessment of the dangers of Nazism, was posted to Rome. This meant the recognition of the conquest of Ethiopia, but was intended to maintain the link with Hitler through Mussolini. On 30th November Mussolini staged a demonstration to humiliate France when the deputies in the Italian parliament greeted the new Ambassador by rising to their feet and shouting a claim to 'Tunisia! Nice! Corsica!' In response Daladier recaptured some of his old fire and made a tour of the south of France, speaking bravely, for what that was worth, of the defence of the French empire.

A few days later Bonnet took the opportunity to 'cement' Franco-German co-operation in a declaration signed with Ribbentrop, the German Foreign Minister. In doing so he was catching up with the British, for when Chamberlain returned from Munich he brought with him not only the Munich agreement but also a declaration which he and Hitler had signed in which 'We, the German Führer and the British Prime Minister' expressed their agreement that 'the question of Anglo-German relations is of the first importance for the two countries and for Europe', and that relations between them should proceed by way of consultation. The Franco-German Declaration, dated 6th December 1938, followed the same form. The occasion had a bad taste to it. It had been preceded early in November by the murder of a minor German diplomat in the embassy in Paris and was taken as the pretext for an orgy of persecution of Jews in Germany. The two Jewish members of the French cabinet were not invited to the reception for Ribbentrop. Nor was it clear how far Bonnet's promises had gone beyond the formal text of the Declaration — Ribbentrop maintained that he had received a private assurance that France would disinterest herself in Eastern and Central Europe.

Left: 1939 French cartoon — Hitler wonders whether to ignore future Nazi targets as 'sour grapes' in the face of threats from Great Britain's Neville Chamberlain and Daladier of France

123

In a different sense France had become uninterested in Central Europe. The British people, perversely, became concerned about Czechoslovakia from the moment that they had connived at its dismemberment. It had indeed, in Chamberlain's words, been a far away country of which they knew nothing, or at least very little. After Munich they contributed more than £400,000 to the Lord Mayor's fund for Czech refugees and bought hundreds of thousands of copies of 'Penguin Specials' on *Europe and the Czechs*. There was no similar reaction in France.

Nor did French opinion follow the same reaction as British to the events that followed Munich—even the final destruction of Czechoslovakia in March 1939. Public opinion in Britain recovered from the mood of relief which had greeted the settlement. In France the mood of defeatism made any similar revision of judgment much smaller in scale.

Nonetheless, a combination of Daladier's hankering after a policy of firmness and Bonnet's desire to direct conflict away from France brought active participation in the diplomacy which followed the occupation of Prague in March 1939. It was French pressure that precipitated the British guarantee to Rumania, and the French played an active part in the attempt to secure an Anglo-Russian guarantee of Poland and Rumania and to activate, at last, the Franco-Russian alliance.

But as the possibility of war grew ever greater, with increasing German pressure on Danzig and Poland, Bonnet outdid Neville Chamberlain in his attempt to produce another conference which might find a way out. His policy remained consistent, now as at Munich: to arrive at any settlement which would avoid war. Chamberlain was prepared to go to almost any lengths to keep the door open to compromise. When Germany invaded Poland on 1st September he expressed his willingness to act as if German troops had never entered Poland, provided they now withdrew. But the House of Commons became increasingly impatient. Meanwhile Bonnet pleaded for more time, for the attempt to avoid war. In the end the British ultimatum to Germany expired at 11 a.m. on 3rd September, the French six hours later.

FRANCE

Population
Each symbol represents
1 million men
Figures in thousands

41,600

National income
Figures in $ millions

10,296

Peacetime armies + Reserves
Each symbol represents
1 million soldiers
Figures in millions

5.2

Aircraft (first line)
Each symbol represents
500 aircraft

600

Destroyers
Each symbol represents
10 destroyers

28

Submarines
Each symbol represents
10 submarines

70

Right: The military balance of power on the outbreak of war

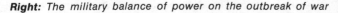

The Balance of Power, 1939

GREAT BRITAIN	POLAND	GERMANY	ITALY
47,692	34,662	68,424	43,779
23,550	3,189	33,347	6,895
0.62	1.79	3.0	5.6
2,075	390	4,500	1,500
184	4	17	60
58	5	56	100

POPULATION PARISIENNE
DIRECTION SUD
Orléans
DIRECTION EST
LILAS
DIRECTION OUEST
CHATILLON
Trappes, Dreux
DAUPHINE
DIRECTION SUD
CHOISY
CHAMPERRET
Argenteuil
Poissy, Meulan
CLICHY
ITALIE

Chapter 7

The End of the Third Republic

The military performance of Britain and France in the opening stages of the war was markedly similar. Neither was prepared to take the offensive. Gamelin, the French Commander-in-Chief, had given an undertaking to the Poles that France would launch a major offensive within the first two weeks of the war to provide relief to Poland, but his commitment never had the formal sanction of his government and his strategy was not designed to implement it. The 'major offensive' was attenuated into nothing more than patrol activity while German tanks and aeroplanes crushed the Polish armed forces.

But the different political and moral experience of the two countries began to appear in these first months. With the conclusion of the Nazi-Soviet Pact and the invasion by Russia of eastern Poland, in accordance with the secret protocol attached to the Pact, the French Communist Party, like other Communist parties, abandoned overnight the attitude of resistance to Germany which had ensured its vote against the Munich agreement. The first effect was to discredit the Party gravely and lead many of its outstanding members to withdraw from it. This was followed by a repressive policy by Daladier's government. The Party was dissolved, the parliamentary immunity of deputies was suspended, and thirty-five of them were imprisoned. Maurice Thorez deserted from the army to escape arrest, was deprived of his citizenship, and took refuge in Russia.

From now until the invasion of Russia by Germany in June 1941 the Communists denounced the war as imperialist and capitalist—as they denounced de Gaulle for carrying on resistance for the benefit of financial interests in Paris. To that extent the Communists had excluded themselves from France at war, and earned the contempt of men of integrity like Léon Blum. Nonetheless Daladier's action was that of a scared and vindictive man. The Communist Party went underground, *L'Humanité* was published clandestinely, there were a

Left: 2nd September 1939—in the Place de l'Opéra Parisians study mobilisation and evacuation orders on the eve of war

few examples of sabotage for which Communists were responsible. Meanwhile, the manner in which action was taken against the Communists brought grim forebodings of the future. Indiscriminately the police rounded up those whom they regarded as suspicious—even when they were in fact refugees from Hitler's Germany or men like the writer Arthur Koestler who had left the Communist Party in disgust over the Spanish Civil War, only to be put in a French concentration camp.

A frenetic hostility to Communism took the French government nearer than the British to entering on a war with Russia at the same time as Germany. While the 'phoney war' continued in the West the Soviet Union attacked Finland in order to establish a forward defence on Finnish territory in front of Leningrad. In both Britain and France their action evoked a wave of solidarity with the Finns which had never arisen in response to Hitler's aggression. Daladier, with strong parliamentary support, pressed the Norwegians and Swedes to permit the passage of troops and supplies to Finland. Their refusal saved Britain and France from this act of folly; but Daladier was so far committed that the collapse of Finnish resistance brought the fall of his government.

The change was comparable to that by which Winston Churchill replaced Chamberlain two months later. It brought to the premiership Paul Reynaud, who had distinguished himself by his political courage and by his determination to prosecute the war with all possible vigour. A small man, he had the bravery and assertiveness that often accompany a short stature. But his political position differed totally from that of Churchill. He had played his part in the political games of the Third Republic and had not built up a party following, far less the almost total popular support which Churchill would command. He lacked the authority in the country which Churchill retained, for all the mistakes of his peacetime politics. This political weakness showed in his construction of a government. In order to have sufficient votes in the Chamber he was unable to dispense with Daladier; his inclusion of him had none of the magnanimity with which Churchill kept Neville Chamberlain. Because of Daladier he could not dismiss Gamelin, as he wanted to, since Gamelin was Daladier's favourite as General Georges was his own. He was not even secure in his personal life, since he could neither dismiss nor command his mistress, the Countess Hélène de Portes. A woman whose charms remained incomprehensible and unfelt by the closest observers, she was able to interfere

Right: The Battle of France—tanks of Rommel's VII Panzer Division pause during their lightning thrust across France

persistently and continuously in public affairs, interrupting Reynaud's daily work, reading and losing documents of the highest secrecy, arranging appointments and dominating his secretaries. None of this need necessarily have been disastrous for France had Hélène de Portes shared Reynaud's determination. On the contrary she was as defeatist as he was resolute and intrigued to further the cause of her defeatist friends.

Meanwhile the respite of the phoney war was not used to advantage. Ordinary soldiers became demoralised and officers behaved like civil servants. Nothing was done to improve a system of command which was neither sufficiently rigorous in its hierarchy nor loose enough to encourage individual independence and initiative. The only exception was that Gamelin, whose command extended over the whole empire, deputed command over the vital north-eastern sector to Georges, thus establishing an alibi for himself once the fighting started in earnest.

The Allies shattered

Once it did so, on 10th May 1940, the onslaught of the German army broke the British and French armies at every one of their many weak points. German tanks showed that the Ardennes, far from being unsuitable for armoured warfare, provided ideal cover for panzer movement in a sector where the Maginot Line did not exist. Belgian neutrality made it impossible for British and French troops to advance into Belgium before the German attack began. When it did, the skill and determination of the German army broke the Belgian defences and deprived the British and French of the breathing space on which they thought they could depend. The governments of Britain and France had been preoccupied with air arrangements as they affected the civilian population; now they were confronted with Stuka dive bombers, inefficient in most aspects of aerodynamics but far more accurate than low-level bombers in their support of ground operations. Vulnerable to men with anti-aircraft guns who stood their ground, they were deeply unnerving to those whose confidence was shaken and who lacked defensive weapons.

In ten days the French army was broken. On 18th May Paul Reynaud reshaped his cabinet in an attempt to re-establish morale and to hold ground. He brought into his cabinet Marshal Philippe Pétain—a man of eighty-four who, in the First World War, had halted the German advance at the historic battle of Verdun. At the same time Gamelin was dismissed. His sensitive appreciation

Right: French refugees flee before the German onslaught

of Italian painting and the fineness of his literary taste had given him an intellectual detachment which was singularly inappropriate to his responsibilities, either to the men under his command or to the destiny of his nation. He was replaced by General Weygand, who was brought home from a command in Syria.

These two men, Reynaud hoped, would show French determination and would stiffen resistance. The mythology associated with the name of Pétain appeared to suit the needs of the moment – phrases such as 'they shall not pass' came to mind. Weygand too had fought in the First World War alongside the great Marshal Foch. In fact the appointments were a mistake. Both men proved to be defeatist – and indeed there was sufficient evidence, at least about Pétain, for Reynaud to know that he believed French participation in the war to have been a mistake, and that it was now lost. Three weeks later the government was again reorganised. Daladier was at last dropped and de Gaulle was brought in as under-secretary for war – but it was too late for him to exercise any influence within the government.

The military situation rapidly passed out of control. On 10th June Italy joined the war on the side of Germany – with great caution, for even at this stage Mussolini was fearful for his troops in North Africa who might be attacked by the British from Egypt. On the same day the government left Paris for Tours, then, on the 15th, went to Bordeaux – the town which seemed furthest from the German advance and at the same time open to the Atlantic and so to Britain.

The decision to leave Paris rather than to fight in the streets of the capital itself showed a weakness of will. But it still left open the momentous decision of whether to make peace or, in some way, to continue the war. In view of the divisions which had been manifest over the previous decade it is not surprising that both decisions were taken, by different groups of Frenchmen.

The decision involved not only France but also Britain – and a calculation, from the French point of view, of the British future. On 28th March the two countries had signed an agreement not to conclude a separate peace or armistice. On 10th May Churchill replaced Chamberlain and the reserve which the British had shown towards France disappeared. As the situation on the battle front became ever more serious Churchill flew five times to

Right: German cartoon of 10th September 1939 portrays Daladier and Chamberlain almost swamped by events. *Next page:* After their victory, Germans patrol Paris. *Page 136:* 'France has lost a battle! But France has not lost the war!' De Gaulle attempts to rouse the spirit of resistance among the French

A TOUS LES FRANÇAIS

La France a perdu une bataille!
Mais la France n'a pas perdu la guerre!

Des gouvernants de rencontre ont pu capituler, cédant à la panique, oubliant l'honneur, livrant le pays à la servitude. Cependant, rien n'est perdu!

Rien n'est perdu, parce que cette guerre est une guerre mondiale. Dans l'univers libre, des forces immenses n'ont pas encore donné. Un jour, ces forces écraseront l'ennemi. Il faut que la France, ce jour-la, soit présente à la victoire. Alors, elle retrouvera sa liberté et sa grandeur. Tel est mon but, mon seul but!

Voila pourquoi je convie tous les Francais, où qu'ils se trouvent, à s'unir à moi dans l'action, dans le sacrifice et dans l'espérance.

Notre patrie est en peril de mort.
Luttons tous pour la sauver!

VIVE LA FRANCE !

C. de Gaulle

GÉNÉRAL DE GAULLE

QUARTIER-GÉNÉRAL,
4, CARLTON GARDENS,
LONDON, S.W.1.

TO ALL FRENCHMEN..

France has lost a battle!
But France has not lost the war!

A makeshift Government may have capitulated, giving way to panic, forgetting honour, delivering their country into slavery. Yet nothing is lost!

Nothing is lost, because this war is a world war. In the free universe immense forces have not yet been brought into play. Some day these forces will crush the enemy. On that day France must be present at the Victory. She will then regain her liberty and her greatness.

That is my goal, my only goal!

That is why I ask all Frenchmen, wherever they may be, to unite with me in action, in sacrifice and in hope.

Our Country is in danger of death. Let us fight to save it!

LONG LIVE FRANCE!

C. de Gaulle

GÉNÉRAL de GAULLE
HEADQUARTERS,
4, CARLTON GARDENS, LONDON, S.W.1.

France. On 16th May he saw the French leaders in Paris, and discovered that 'the situation was incomparably worse than we had imagined'. (It was on this occasion that Gamolin, as if giving a classroom lecture, calmly outlined the state of the battle, without making any proposals for action and then, when asked by Churchill where the strategic reserve was, replied 'None'.) Ten days later he was back, and was heartened by the change which seemed to have taken place – by Reynaud's resolve and by the spirit of Weygand. His last visit was on 13th June, when the French army had been given the order for a general retreat and Reynaud asked to be released from the commitment not to sign a separate armistice.

For all the dismay caused by what he saw and what he learned from General Spears, whom he had sent as his special representative to Reynaud, Churchill used the full force of his personality to persuade the French to continue the fight – to defend Paris, and in the end not to give in. His government finally (on 16th June) agreed to the French government making a separate enquiry about armistice conditions – provided that the French fleet sailed to British ports. Immediately afterwards it proposed that an 'indissoluble union' should be formed between the two nations, which would thus 'no longer be two nations, but one Franco-British Union. . . . Every citizen of France will enjoy immediately citizenship of Great Britain; every British subject will become a citizen of France.'

Perfidious Albion?
But while Churchill urged the French towards resolution and defiance – and succeeded in bringing new courage to Reynaud – he had no choice but to preserve British forces intact for the continuance of the common struggle. On 16th May he heartened Reynaud by offering six extra fighter squadrons to operate in France and give air support in defence against the German panzers; but on his return to England he had to concede that they could neither be put at risk given the need for the defence of Britain, nor could they operate from the diminishing number of French airfields. They remained, instead, in the south of England. In the same way it was the British army, in much larger strength than the French, which was able to escape from Dunkirk, thanks to the command of Lord Gort and the way in which the British had been deployed in the battle.

British action was thus open to recrimination by those who did not want to believe that Churchill's government had the common interests of the two countries at heart. And for some, hostility went very much deeper. At best the defeatists were unwilling to believe that Britain

would survive to continue the battle—they were all too ready to believe that British defeat must follow soon after that of the French. At worst there were those who shared Laval's hope that the British would be defeated. Franco, said Laval, 'had suffered too often as a result of British dishonesty and hypocrisy'.

But although British action and the interpretation which Frenchmen gave to it was of great importance, the decision which they had to take concerned France and was determined by their view of the future of France. As the effect of military defeat came to be felt, so the strength of those who wanted to arrive at terms with Germany increased. In the first place they had been given a leader by the appointment of Pétain and his consequent avail-ability to lead the defeatist party. His record and his prestige gave it respectability; at the same time the ver-dict of Weygand on the military aspect made it easier to argue that there was no choice but to accept defeat. The arguments which they used were essentially those of defensive nationalism. They were too insular to believe that they could be responsible for the future of France once they left the country. They could persuade them-selves—the more easily since they assumed that Britain would be defeated—that they must protect France by remaining on French territory and negotiating with Hitler. In varying degrees they were complacent about Hitler's intentions and the ability of France to survive as a nation within the framework of Hitler's new order in Europe.

The French overseas
Not least surprising in the attitude of these men was their unwillingness to continue the battle from the terri-tory of overseas France. For France stood, at this time, at the centre of a large empire, including Indo-China and the mandated territories of Syria and Lebanon. Closest to metropolitan France were the North African terri-tories of Tunisia, Algeria, and Morocco and, to the south, the vast area of Equatorial and West Africa. The struc-ture of the French Empire was different from the British Commonwealth in that there were no independent Dominions like Australia and Canada. This was partly because there had not been a large French emigration, partly because the assumption on which colonial policy had been based was that the overseas territories should be assimilated as closely as possible to France. As a result of this policy the coastal departments of Algeria had become departments of France, sending deputies to the

Left: German soldiers survey their enemies' conquered capital

Chamber of Deputies and governed from Paris.

Amongst the resisters there was a strong move to take the government to North Africa. After the fall of Reynaud's government an unlucky band of parliamentarians set out on the *Massilia* to Algeria. They included Mandel, Daladier, Jean Zay, Pierre Mendès-France. But the only effect of their voyage was to remove them from the scene while an armistice was signed. They were not allowed to be effective in Algeria, where the administration was in the hands of the Pétain supporter General Noguès, nor could Mandel get in touch with Duff Cooper or Lord Gort whom Churchill sent to make contact with them.

The stability of the French Empire was by no means secure. The 1930s had seen the growth of nationalist movements in all the major overseas territories, but particularly in Syria and Lebanon, Tunisia and Morocco. The governments of the Third Republic had been slow to introduce constitutional change to meet nationalist demands. Reforms which Blum proposed during his first government remained a dead letter since they were rejected by the Chamber. The colonial administrators and the military had, in general, been the most resistant to ideas of reform and had claimed to be safeguarding French interests. But when defeat came on the mainland the majority of those in charge of the colonial territories sided with the government of Pétain. They resisted an attempt by de Gaulle to establish his Free French forces at Dakar as they would have resisted him in North Africa and Syria were not the invasions of those countries carried out by overwhelming forces of American, British, and Commonwealth troops. Only in Central Africa was General Leclerc able to re-form a Free French army, and then march northwards to join the Allied armies in the battle for North Africa.

The fate of the overseas territories was linked to that of the fleet, and it was to this that Churchill attached most importance when he no longer hoped for effective military resistance. He took care to draw aside its commanding admiral, Darlan, during one of his last visits to France and to say how ardently he hoped that he would never let the fleet fall into the hands of the Germans. Darlan was a proud sailor who commanded the loyalty of his service; but he had no love for England. His great-grandfather (as he told Churchill) was killed at Trafalgar, and his attitude was typical of that of many French naval officers who inherited a strong sense of rivalry with the British. Even so the fate of the fleet might have been different had not Pétain offered Darlan the Ministry of the Marine — a post which the Admiral had coveted all his life. He then miscalculated the future. He could have sailed with his fleet to join the British and so become the

unquestioned commander of a strong independent French force which would carry the tricolour through to victory. Instead he believed that his ambition and the interests of France coincided, that he should remain to protect the fleet from the Germans. In the event the only way in which it could be so protected was by being scuttled, in 1942, in the harbour at Toulon; Darlan himself was assassinated in North Africa after the Anglo-American invasion, on Christmas Eve of the same year.

Meanwhile there were other factors at work in Bordeaux to strengthen the cause of the defeatists. As a haven for the government the town was geographically well chosen. But it so happened that its mayor, Adrien Marquet, was an old friend of Laval. As soon as the government moved Laval left his home at Châteldon and joined Marquet. He set up an office in the town hall, and as deputies and senators arrived began organising those who shared his views and converting those who did not. Parliament had been reduced to a very low order by the conduct of government through decree laws; now, in Bordeaux, there was no attempt to call the two houses together, although their presidents were there. Deputies and senators were the more vulnerable to the intrigue of the defeatists.

The government received no support from parliament, nor was it stiffened by the attitude of the President of the Republic. President Lebrun had been re-elected a year before—breaking precedent, since a president normally only served for one seven-year term. Potentially his office was one of importance, in spite of the fact that it had more often than not been held by older politicians, virtually in retirement. But Lebrun was not the man to step into the gap created by a national emergency. He took events as they came.

A separate peace

And increasingly they moved towards armistice. Reynaud hoped to find a way out by having the army order a cease-fire so that fighting could stop without the government of France having to make peace—the course of action which the Dutch had followed. Weygand refused, saying that the honour of the army would not allow it. Meanwhile Chautemps, producing again the skill of manipulation which had earned him his reputation in the parliamentary game, suggested that it was worth at least asking for armistice terms, so that if they proved too harsh, the people of France would see that the government had no choice but to refuse. It was an insidious

Left: Daladier in the last days of his premiership. He was shortly to be interned by Pétain (seen on the extreme right)

formula which salved some consciences. It was now that Reynaud asked the British to release France from the agreement not to make a separate peace. His hopes that the reply would be negative were unfulfilled; and although he welcomed the proposal for Franco-British union it was greeted by the defeatists as an attempt by Britain to take over France. Still, Reynaud refused himself to implement Chautemps' proposal. At this decisive moment Lebrun asked Pétain to form a new government. On 17th June he broadcast to the French people telling them that he was seeking an armistice. Three hours earlier de Gaulle had returned to England with General Spears. As Churchill said, he 'carried with him, in this small aeroplane, the honour of France'. On 18th June he broadcast from London—few Frenchmen heard him, since they were not tuned to BBC: 'France is not alone. She has a vast empire behind her. She can unite with the British Empire, which holds the seas, and is continuing the struggle. She can utilise to the full, as England is doing, the vast industrial resources of the United States.

'I, General de Gaulle, invite French officers and officers who are in Britain . . . to put themselves in touch with me. . . .

'Whatever happens, the flame of French resistance must never go out and will never go out.'

Hitler knew what was at stake in the negotiations for an armistice. Now as before he showed his awareness of the attitude of those Frenchmen likely to negotiate with him. He subjected them to the humiliation of signing an armistice on the same spot, in the same railway carriage as had been used for the armistice of 1918, when France was the victor. But the terms of the armistice, which provided for the occupation of only the northern and eastern part of France, were acceptable to men who believed that it was their duty to save what could be saved by staying in France, with the vast majority of their people, as a buttress against the invader. But these men had no wish to protect the constitution of the Third Republic. On the contrary, the antipathy of the Right to the parliamentary regime, their bitter hostility to the Popular Front which it had produced, mingled with the defeatism and pacifism of some of the Left to bring, on 10th July, the end of the Third Republic. Philippe Pétain became, not president, but Chief of the French State; Pierre Laval was nominated his successor. The government was established at the health resort of Vichy, in the unoccupied zone of France.

How much was saved by Pétain's armistice, in terms of reprisals which might have been exacted, cruelties which

Right: *Guardians of a defeated nation—the premier, Marshal Philippe Pétain (right), and Admiral Jean Louis Darlan at Vichy*

might have been inflicted on a population had there been no government to make peace, it is impossible to tell. History can only record that in seeking to defend a certain concept of France the Vichy government opened the way to those elements of French society which in the 1930s had shown most sympathy with Germany and saw the murder in 1944 of Georges Mandel by the Vichy forces of order while Léon Blum and his wife were taken to prison in Germany. The partial occupation came to an end with the Anglo-American attack on North Africa in 1942, when German troops occupied the whole country to fore-stall a possible invasion from the south and the Vichy government was forced into a position of increasing collaboration with the Germans.

The leadership which de Gaulle, by his simple audacity, had offered from London alone could provide the central core of the Resistance. Subject to the normal strains of a government in exile, he nonetheless created a unity amongst men of widely differing political opinions, in-spired and motivated by a conviction in the future of their country. Victory, when it was won, did not immediately make it possible to restore this same unity to France as a whole. Still a mocrocosm of world politics, she was sub-jected to the harsh divisions of the cold war and endured the long drawn-out and wasteful war of decolonisation in Indo-China and Algeria. But her creativity within the European movement was to return in the 1950s, her independence as a major power would be regained and her sense of nationhood restored.

Right: End of the Third Republic—the map of defeated France

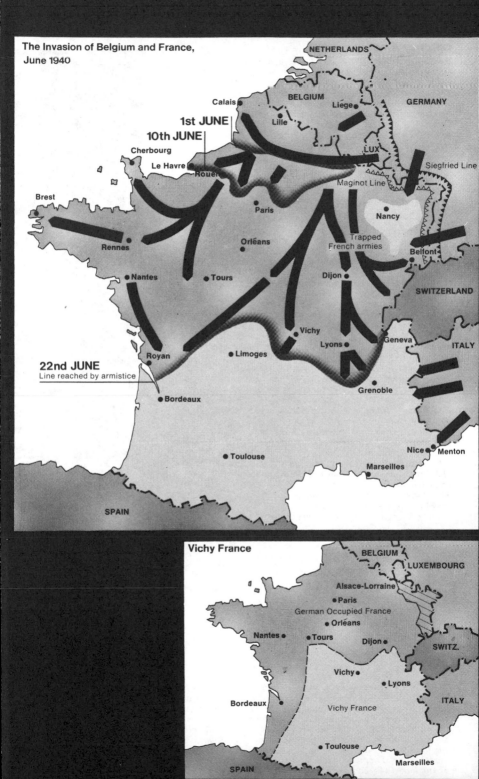

The Invasion of Belgium and France, June 1940

NETHERLANDS
BELGIUM
GERMANY
Calais
Liège
Lille
1st JUNE
10th JUNE
LUX
Cherbourg
Le Havre
Siegfried Line
Rouen
Maginot Line
Brest
Nancy
Paris
Trapped
French armies
Rennes
Orléans
Belfort
Nantes
Tours
Dijon
SWITZERLAND
Vichy
22nd JUNE
Line reached by armistice
Royan
Limoges
Lyons
Geneva
ITALY
Grenoble
Bordeaux
Nice
Menton
Toulouse
Marseilles
SPAIN

Vichy France

BELGIUM
LUXEMBOURG
Alsace-Lorraine
Paris
German Occupied France
Orléans
Nantes
Tours
Dijon
SWITZ.
Vichy
Lyons
Bordeaux
ITALY
Vichy France
Toulouse
Marseilles
SPAIN

Chronology of Events

1934 **8th January:** Serge-Alexandre Stavisky found dead.
6th February: Right-wing leagues attempt a coup d'état in Paris.
8th February: Gaston Doumergue becomes premier.
9th October: Foreign Minister Louis Barthou and King Alexander of Jugoslavia assassinated in Marseilles.

1935 **January:** Saar votes for reunion with Germany.
April: Stresa Pact between France, Britain, and Italy.
2nd May: Franco-Soviet Pact concluded.
September: Italy invades Ethiopia.
28th December: Leagues ordered to dissolve.

1936 **7th March:** Germany re-militarises the Rhineland.
3rd May: Popular Front wins the elections to parliament.
5th June: First Popular Front government formed under Socialist Léon Blum.
18th July: Beginning of Spanish Civil War.
2nd October: Devaluation of the franc.

1937 **March:** Blum announces a 'breathing spell' in the work of social reform.
June: Fall of Blum government, succeeded by Radical leader Camille Chautemps.

1938 **March:** *Anschluss* — Austria becomes a province of the German *Reich.*
April: Edouard Daladier becomes premier.
September: Munich crisis.

1939 **February:** France recognises Franco's fascist government in Spain.
March: Germany occupies all of Czechoslovakia: Anglo-French guarantee to Poland.
21st August: Announcement of Nazi-Soviet Pact.
1st September: Germany invades Poland.
3rd September: Britain and France declare war on Germany.
26th September: Daladier dissolves French Communist Party.

1940 **20th March:** Paul Reynaud succeeds Daladier as premier.
10th May: Germany invades Low Countries.
14th May: French front broken on the Meuse.
29th May-4th June: Dunkirk evacuation.
14th June: Germans enter Paris.
16th June: Reynaud resigns: Philippe Pétain succeeds him.
18th June: General de Gaulle calls from London for continued French resistance.
22nd June: Armistice with Germany.
24th June: Armistice with Italy.
1st July: French government moves to Vichy.

A COCK-AND-BEAR STORY.

LE CANCER

Top: Early Popular Front demonstration (left); July 1936 — new premier Léon Blum addresses a rally (centre); police patrol the Place de la République during a May Day demonstration (right). Centre: Punch cartoon mocks Hitler's protests against the light restraints of the Franco-Soviet Pact (left); 1936 strikers sit-in (centre); Parisians read of Hitler's attack on Poland (right). Bottom: Right-wing propaganda portrays France as the victim of the Communist 'cancer' (left); German spy arrested at Dunkirk, 1940 (centre); French artillery in action (right)

Index of main people, places, and events

Author's suggestions for further reading:

There are several interpretations of the history of the Third French Republic. One of the most successful is still David Thomson, *Democracy in France* (London 1952). The economic history of the period is studied in Alfred Sauvy, *Histoire economique de la France entre les deux guerres* vol. II 1931-39 (Paris 1967). Two recent histories of political parties provide valuable accounts of the political scene as a whole, as well as a detailed examination of their subject. They are Peter J. Larmour, *The French Radical Party in the 1930s* (Stanford 1964) and Nathanael Greene, *Crisis and decline, the French Socialist Party in the Popular Front era* (Cornell 1969). A brief analysis of the Leagues and right-wing movements is by S. J. Woolf in the collection, edited S. J. Woolf, *European Fascism* (London 1968). A more exhaustive study of Action Française is in Eugen Weber, *Action française* (Stanford 1962). An excellent biography of Laval has been written by Geoffrey Warner, *Pierre Laval and the eclipse of France* (London 1968). A shorter study of Blum is to be found in James Joll, *Intellectuals in Politics* (London 1968). The defeat of France in 1940 is brilliantly explored by Alistair Horne in *To lose a battle, France 1940* (London 1969). Alexander Werth published several works based on his reports to the *Manchester Guardian* in the 1930s which are still worth reading. They are: *France in Ferment* (London 1935), *Destiny of France* (London 1937), *The Twilight of France 1933-40* (London 1942, reprinted New York 1966).

Library of the 20th Century will include the following titles:

Russia in Revolt
David Floyd
The Second Reich
Harold Kurtz
The Anarchists
Roderick Kedward
Suffragettes International
Trevor Lloyd
War by Time-Table
A.J.P.Taylor
Death of a Generation
Alistair Horne
Suicide of the Empires
Alan Clark
Twilight of the Habsburgs
Z.A.B.Zeman
Early Aviation
Sir Robert Saundby
Birth of the Movies
D.J.Wenden
America Comes of Age
A.E.Campbell
Lenin's Path to Power
G.Katkov/H.Shukman
Weimar Germany
Sefton Delmer
Out of the Lion's Paw
Constantine FitzGibbon
Japan: The Years of Triumph
Louis Allen
Communism Takes China
C.P.FitzGerald
Black and White in South Africa
G.H.Le May
Woodrow Wilson
Edmund Ions
France 1918-34
J.P.T.Bury
France 1934-40
W.Knapp
Mussolini's Italy
Esmonde Robertson
The Little Dictators
A.Polonsky
Viva Zapata
L.Bethell
The World Depression
Malcolm Falkus
Stalin's Russia
A.Nove
The Brutal Reich
Donald Watt
The Spanish Civil War
Raymond Carr
Munich: Czech Tragedy
K.G.Robbins

Wilfrid Knapp read PPE at New College, Oxford, and is now Fellow and Tutor in Politics at St Catherine's, Oxford. He is the author of *A History of War and Peace, 1939-65* and *Tunisia.*

J M Roberts, General Editor of the Macdonald *Library of the 20th Century,* is Fellow and Tutor in Modern History at Merton College, Oxford. He was also General Editor of Purnell's *History of the 20th Century,* and is Joint-Editor of the *English Historical Review* and author of *Europe 1880-1945* in the Longmans History of Europe. He has been English Editor of the Larousse Encyclopedia of Modern History, has reviewed for *The Observer, New Statesman,* and *Spectator,* and given talks on the BBC.

Library of the 20th Century

Editor: Richard Johnson
Executive Editor: Peter Prince
Designed by: Brian Mayers/ Germano Facetti
Design: HCB Designs
Research: Gun Brinson/Evan Davies/Germano Facetti

Pictures selected from the following sources:

Archiv Gerstenberg 114
Archives Rencontre 8 24 90 111 120
Bibliothèque Nationale Paris 28 54
Rene Dazy 22 147
Galerie Beyerle Basle 20
Giraudon 19 38
L'Illustration 13 27 35 42 46 58
Imperial War Museum 129
Institute for Contemporary History Amsterdam 78 102
Keystone 152
Lords Gallery 40 136
Musée de L'Art Moderne Paris 17
Popperfoto 31 83 85 93 104
Punch 62 146
Radio Times Hulton 44
Sado 13
Simplicissimus 133
Snark International Cover 37 80 97 99 138
Spadem 100
Sphere 116
Suddeutscher Verlag 71 72 89
Ullstein 53 89
Roger Viollet 4 8 9 12 14 32 48 65 66 68 74 87 113 143 146 147
Wiener Library 1 57 77 98 146